Praise for *The Lantern Man*

"*The Lantern Man* is an extraordinary novel that defies categorization. With shades of Stephen King, *Silence of the Lambs*, journalism, and author Jon Bassoff's own groundbreaking vision of how to use the printed page to give readers the best story possible, *The Lantern Man* is a landmark novel that will make you wonder, marvel, and remember."

—James Grady, author of
Six Days of the Condor

"*The Lantern Man* is disorienting in the best sense of the word. Jon Bassoff masterfully blurs the lines between genres—no, scratch that, *among* genres—by creating a hellish hall of competing mirrors, each holding its own twisted version of the truth. *The Lantern Man* is a true shape-shifter of a novel. It's one that will remain with readers long after the last page."

—Lynn Kostoff, author of
Words to Die For

"*The Lantern Man* is a brilliant—and terrifying—puzzle-box narrative that dares you to keep reading. It's the kind of book that you better cancel any plans you might have before you start."

—Rob Hart, author of
The Warehouse

"An engaging and immersive mashup of mystery and horror, Jon Bassoff's *The Lantern Man* offers a dizzying world of clues interlacing the disappearances of several girls with the mythology of a local boogeyman. Bassoff weaves a tight and creepy tale through a series of mediums: a girl's diary, police transcripts, a detective's notes, newspaper articles, letters, photos, and sketches. The result is an exceptionally creative, compelling, and dark whodunit that will leave its readers, like the Lantern Man himself, hungry for more."

—Carter Wilson,
USA Today bestselling author

"Ever been eyebrows deep in a horrifying investigation? You're about to be...Part memoir, part case file and completely absorbing, *The Lantern Man* is a compelling pastiche on the verge of madness."

—Craig Johnson, author of
the Walt Longmire mysteries

"A genre-bending novel—an original, captivating mystery that might pave the way we write crime fiction forever."

—Jax Miller, author of
Freedom's Child

The Lantern Man

The Lantern Man

A Novel

Jon Bassoff

Down & Out Books
3959 Van Dyke Road, Suite 265
Lutz, FL 33558
DownAndOutBooks.com

Cover design by Matthew Revert
Interior art by Cole Brenner

ISBN: 1-64396-076-8
ISBN-13: 978-1-64396-076-0

For Leah,
One of the good ones.

"Let the guilty bury the innocent,
and let no one change the evidence."
—Ian McEwan, *Atonement*

Leadville Tol

$1.00   June 6, 2008

Local Girl Found Dead

by Caleb Walford

LEADVILLE — A local girl has been reported dead, the result of a cabin fire in the woods outside of Leadville.

Seventeen-year-old Lizzy Greiner had been missing since Monday when her mother reported that she hadn't come home after school. On Friday, a fire broke out in the old Smith House located in the ghost town of Douglass City. Firemen were called upon the scene to put out the fire, and when they entered the cabin they found the remains of a body which was later identified as Lizzy. It is believed that she had been sleeping in the cabin for several days before the fire started.

The cabin had long since been condemned, but over the last several years it had been used as shelter by vagrants as well as a meeting place for teenagers to drink. It is not known why Lizzy was in the cabin or if there were other people that were staying with her.

Lizzy attended Lake Valley High School in Leadville. She enjoyed hiking, drawing, and writing. Her English teacher, Mary Donovan, described her as a "troubled girl," but explained that she was "incredibly intelligent and one of the most talented writers and artists I've ever taught."

Lizzy Greiner, 17 years old.

Her friend, Tabitha Moore, said that Lizzy had a great sense of humor and a good heart. "She was always making me laugh. But the best thing about her was that she was a genuine friend who looked out for me when I was down."

While the source of the fire is unknown, investigators have not ruled out foul play. Detective Russ Buchanan said, "We will see where this investigation takes us, but right now nothing is off the table."

Lizzy's mother, Jessica Greiner, said she was still having a difficult time believing that her daughter was dead. "I don't know if this is real. I can't believe it. She was my heart. Without her, I don't think I will ever be able to smile or feel happiness again."

Continued on page 2

Locals to learn what it means to be a Leadman/woman

by Mike Dumler

Next time you don't think you can do another leg press at the gym, perhaps you should think about Don Peller of Leadville. It might provide

sure he would run marathons in the foothills over the weekend.

The famous Leadville race series takes place over several weeks of the summer. It includes more than 300 miles of running and biking on rough terrain and about 45,000 feet of elevation

Detective Russ Buchanan
August 15, 2008

Dear Chief Mickel,

I am writing you in regards to the recent death of Lizzy Greiner. As you are aware, her body was recovered and identified this past spring after a fire destroyed the property that she had apparently been squatting in. As you are also aware, several of her journals were recovered at the scene of the crime, having been kept safe in a fireproof box. Forensics has determined that the journals were, in fact, written by Lizzy. To be perfectly clear, the writings seem to read less as a diary and more as an experimental memoir (intriguingly titled "The Lantern Man"), but given the strange circumstances surrounding her death as well as her apparent knowledge regarding the Chloe Peterson case, they are of particular interest to our department. Following the recent suspension of Detective Kline (who had been assigned to the Peterson case), I have been at the forefront in attempting to ascertain the journals' relevance and truthfulness.

Despite the hearsay nature of the documents, I have been assured by legal that the journals can be used as evidence, assuming a factual analysis (see *Bob Packwood, Applicant v Senate Select Committee on Ethics, No. A-704, 1994*). I mention this because after Kline's initial investigation resulted in a pair of arrests, these writings have convinced me of the necessity to reopen both the Peterson and Greiner investigations. While I understand that it might be painful for many to relitigate these crimes and will not be politically expedient, I still subscribe to the Fraternal Order of Police's motto of "Fairness, Justice, Equality." It is our duty, then, to determine the truth and levy justice, even if that truth and justice contradict our original findings.

Of course, there are understandably bound to be concerns about relying too heavily on Lizzy's writings, especially considering her background. Indeed, she was somebody whose life had been impacted terribly by tragedy and who might very well have suffered from acute mental illness (as detailed by her psychiatrist, Dr. Sharon Waugh). But owing to these many doubts of reliability, I have done my best to corroborate or refute all events detailed in her story. Therefore, as you read through Lizzy's narrative (transcribed), I have included my own investigative findings (written as footnotes). I have also included other documents pertaining to the investigation, including photos, letters, newspaper articles, and interviews conducted by myself and Detective Kline. I have placed these various documents not in chronological order, but in an order that I feel makes it easier to understand the circumstances and evidence surrounding the crimes.

After reading, I fully expect that you will authorize the reopening of both cases. I also fully expect that you will continue pledging loyalty to our profession's most sacred entity: Truth.

Sincerely,

Russ Buchanan

Detective Russ Buchanan

PART 1

CHAPTER 1

From the time we were old enough to listen, my father used to tell us the story of the Lantern Man. How he'd been a part of a small crew building an old railroad tunnel back in the 1880s and had gotten trapped deep underground and been left there to freeze to death.[1] "Ever since that time," Dad would say in a voice barely louder than a whisper, "his ghost wanders through the forest each and every night, his lantern bouncing up and down, creating menacing shadows. As he walks, he whistles a single note, unchanging. All the animals take shelter because they know they're near evil. The Lantern Man doesn't eat. He doesn't drink. He searches for children who have strayed too far from the path to keep him eternal company in his cold, abandoned tunnel. He can smell the sweet flesh of children, and so once he finds them he follows them silently, staying hidden behind the boughs of the forest. Eventually, the child is bound to sense that someone is watching her. She'll look around and say, 'Who's there?' But as soon as she stares into his lantern, he releases a hideous scream and races toward her. Sometimes he strangles her. Sometimes he suffocates her. Sometimes he drowns her. Sometimes he burns her. But always he kills her. And when

---

[1] This is likely a reference to the Hagerman Tunnel, which was the highest railroad tunnel at the time of its completion in 1887. Building these types of mountain railroads was very dangerous, so it is conceivable that one or more workers died during the construction.

1

the forest is empty for too long and he is in need of a fresh soul, he sneaks into town. It is always in the wee small hours of the morning when everybody is sleeping, but if you were to glance out your window at the exact right moment, you might see the lantern bouncing up and down, held by a shadowy figure. He waits, he waits. And when the night becomes completely still, he enters a house through cracks in the windows or gaps beneath doors. Upon entering, he stands there for minutes, sometimes an hour or more, just watching them sleep. Children, have you ever had a terrible nightmare? Have you ever shivered in the darkness? That's because the Lantern Man is watching you. He's making up his mind. Should he take you? Is your soul pure? Or does he want another one—the pretty girl down the street? Her mischievous brother? But if he does finally make up his mind to take you, he blows out his lantern first, and then he kisses you on the cheek, just like your daddy would. And your nightmare might end and you might open your eyes, but you won't see anything but darkness. With black magic, he's able to trap boys and girls in a burlap sack; then he races unseen back to the woods."[2]

While he told these tales, Shannon, Stormy, and I would stare at him wide-eyed and open-mouthed. The stories terrified us, of course, yet, strangely, they also provided a kind of comfort, as rituals will do. When he finished telling a story, he would gather us on his lap and laugh and tell us that we would always be safe because if the Lantern Man ever tried to get us, Dad would be waiting with an axe and torch. And so, reassured, we would always beg for another.

Sometimes he told us these stories before bed. Sometimes he told them as we walked through town. One time, while we were eating breakfast at the Golden Burro Café, an old woman over-

---

[2] This seems to be a local version of the boogeyman tale, of which almost every country and culture has an example (see figure 1 for Francisco Goya's painting of the so-called hobgoblin). As far as the Lantern Man is concerned, local campfire stories and late-night tales can be traced back several decades at least (see excerpt from *The Encyclopedia of Monsters, Ghouls, and Ogres*).

heard him telling us about the Lantern Man's collection of shoes and toys and teeth, about the body parts preserved in jars of formaldehyde. The old woman should have minded her own business—after all, each father parents in his own way—but, instead, she rose from her seat, flattened out her dress, and walked over to where we were sitting. She pointed at Dad and said, "Why are you telling these awful stories? You're bound to give these poor children nightmares."

Dad glared at the old woman through narrowed eyes before a smile slowly appeared on his face. "And I hope I do, ma'am. Children need something to be afraid of. Don't you think?"

And Shannon and I, at least, *were* afraid.

Each night, before bedtime, we would duct tape the bottom of our windows and the cracks beneath our shared bedroom door to prevent the Lantern Man's entrance. Shannon collected nails and sharpened stones and stored them beneath her mattress. I slept with my tennis shoes on, just in case I needed to escape quickly.[3]

Even as we got older and our father stopped telling us those stories, we still remembered and we were still afraid.

Everybody says that I, more than Shannon and Stormy, take after my father, and I guess I do. "There's a lot of meanness in people," he used to say, and I couldn't help but agree with him. The way Dad looked at things, he'd always been a prisoner of his own life. That's a hell of a thing. All he ever wanted, he told me once, was to have a real choice. To make his own mistakes. To commit his own sins. But he'd never been given that opportunity. His grandfather, Mark Greiner, was a miner (silver); his father, Dallas Greiner, was a miner (zinc); and so eventually he slipped into that same fate (molybdenum). By the time he was twenty-three, he felt that he was forever trapped in a town

---

[3] When Lizzy's body was discovered, badly charred, the rubber soles from her tennis shoes were melded to her scorched feet.

(Leadville) that he hated, doing a job he hated more. And while he never told me so, I always wondered if he felt the same way about his family.[4]

You see, when my mother was twenty years old, she got pregnant. Not with one baby. And not with two. Upon finding out, Dad shouted a lifetime's worth of obscenities, punched a hole in the wall, and then drove for sixteen hours until he was in California. Only the ocean stopped him from driving more. He didn't know a soul in the state, nor did he have any real desire to live there. After two weeks of sitting around in a flea-bag motel called The Lamplighter, he got back in his car and drove home. According to him, he never shouted at Mom again, and I suppose he did his best to be a good father. Eventually you realize those prison bars aren't melting, and that's the cell you've got to live in.

Shannon, Stormy, and I were born on October 5th, 1990. Shannon and I were identical. Stormy was the singleton. We were always proud about being triplets, owing to how rare it was. But the extrasensory perception stuff you hear about wasn't really the case with us. We didn't know when one of us was in pain. We couldn't read each other's thoughts.

If we could have, then maybe things would have turned out differently.[5]

---

[4] Michael Greiner was arrested three times in his late teens and early twenties for assault (twice) and theft (once). It is unclear whether Lizzy knew about his priors, but even if she did, it is likely that she idealized him enough to forgive him of those transgressions.

[5] This is one of the oddest inconsistencies (lies?) in Lizzy's narrative. While it is true that she and Shannon were twins, the three siblings were not triplets—Stormy was born eleven months prior on November 13, 1989.

Duendecitos.

Figure 1: Caprichos: Hobgoblins (Duendecitos) by Francisco de Goya y Lucientes (1799). © The Norton Simon Foundation.

CHAPTER 2

Right now, I'm remembering. That day. That moment. But memories are faulty, edited each time we recall. The way I figure things, memories don't tell about the past. They tell about the present. And right now, in the present, this is what I recall.

Morning. Summertime. Warm. The sky was the bluest blue and the grass was the greenest green. But were they really? Doubtful. A memory edited. We left early in the morning, Shannon, Stormy, and I, and got on our mountain bikes. We had swimsuits on beneath our clothes, and Stormy had towels in his backpack. It was three miles to Opal Lake, but the road was mountainous, and it took us a long time to get there. The whole time we rode, Shannon kept singing "Don't Cha" by the Pussycat Dolls, and Stormy kept telling her to shut up. But even if he was annoyed, we both knew he wasn't angry. Stormy didn't get angry.

Finally, we got to the lake, the water shimmering with strange images like some Dali painting. High in the mountains, the lake was surrounded by old-growth pine trees, aspen groves, and wildflowers. Giggling, we dropped our bikes behind some mountain shrubs and pulled off our outer clothes. Despite the fact that it was late July, the water was still frigid, so Stormy had to bribe us with promises of jellybeans until we finally stuck in our toes and then our whole bodies. I shrieked from the blast of cold, but it didn't take long to become acclimated.

For the next two hours at least, the three of us swam and shouted and laughed, and it was an idyllic day and an idyllic childhood. Nobody else was there, and we had the whole lake to ourselves.

Stormy was a really good swimmer, so he'd recently had the stupid idea of trying out for the swim team. At some point, he left us to go practice the butterfly, swimming far out toward the middle of the lake before turning around and coming back to shore. Shannon and I, meanwhile, were more cautious and remained in the shallower water where our feet could touch the bottom.

Having nothing else to do, we decided to have a competition on who could stay underwater the longest. My first time under, I held my breath for thirty-eight seconds. Not bad. But Shannon had always been competitive and wasn't going to let me win. She made it to forty-five before her head popped above the surface. I called her a bitch—just playing, of course. Then I tried again. Forty-seven seconds. I thought I was going to explode. It was a new record that, I figured, would never be broken. But, like I said, Shannon was uber competitive (maybe owing to the fact that she was officially the youngest, having been born twenty minutes after me and forty minutes after Stormy). Back under she went, sucking the air into her lungs and bobbing beneath the surface of the water. I counted out loud. Thirty. Forty. Fifty. A minute! Still she didn't come up. And it was at that point that I felt an inexplicable sense of dread. Felt that she'd be swallowed up by the tide, never to be seen again. A dread that is now a constant. But a moment before I prepared to dive after my sister, my identical DNA, Shannon's head popped above the surface and she released her breath and then laughed an exhilarated laugh. "How long?" she said. And then again. "How long? That's gotta be a record."

I nodded my head. I had to give her credit. "Yup. A record. Seventy-two seconds."

"I thought I was going to die," Shannon said. "I really did."

I don't remember what we did next. Ate a snack, maybe. Swam some more, probably. After another hour or so, I became tired and wanted to go home. But Stormy was back out in the lake, this time doing the backstroke, and Shannon had no desire to leave. "We could stay here forever, don't you think?" I pulled myself along the sandy bottom of the lake until I reached the shore. Shivering, I wrapped myself in a towel and sat down on a long rock.

Shannon, meanwhile, called out for Stormy who was maybe a hundred yards from shore. He didn't seem to hear her and just continued swimming, his head occasionally appearing above the surface as he took in a breath. Shannon waded farther into the lake before pushing forward into a slow breaststroke/doggy paddle.[6]

Meanwhile, I hunched forward on the rock, still trying to warm up, savoring a moment of relative solitude. The sun was now high in the sky and reflected brilliantly off the water. I touched my shoulders and noticed that they were hot, the start, maybe, of a summer's sunburn. I removed my towel and rose to my feet, the dirt scraping against the soft underside of my feet. To see my brother and sister better, I shielded my eyes from the sun. Stormy was taking a moment's break by treading water. Then he took a deep breath and continued toward the shore, where I stood. But where was Shannon? I took a few steps forward until the water lapped over my feet. I finally spotted her not fifteen yards from Stormy. She seemed to be facing the shore, but it was difficult to tell if she was swimming or just treading water. Shannon raised her arm and waved. Hello? Or help? I took a few more steps into the water. Then I watched as

---

[6] By all accounts, Shannon was a reasonably capable swimmer. Jessica Greiner claimed that her daughter was in swimming lessons for two years when she was in elementary school. To her knowledge, she never expressed any fear about going into the water.

Shannon's head disappeared. I waited a few moments, unsure. Shannon's head reappeared for a moment and then vanished again. Stormy didn't seem to notice that she had been swimming toward him. He had passed his sister and was nearing the shore, nearing where I stood. When the water was shallow enough, he stood and faced me, a big grin on his face. "Not bad, huh?" he said. Then, "Where's Shannon?"

My expression must have revealed terror. Stormy turned back toward the lake where Shannon's hands could now be seen thrashing at the water.

For several moments, Stormy and I stood there in a collective paralysis. Then Stormy shouted her name, but his voice was frail. Without waiting further, he dove back into the water, ignoring the exhaustion from his recent swim. But I didn't move. *Dread.* I couldn't.

Stormy was swimming as quickly as he could, but it seemed that he wasn't moving at all. His arms must have been heavy and he was gasping for air. And now perhaps he was disoriented, unsure of where he had last seen Shannon thrashing.

I was counting out loud. "Sixty, sixty-one, sixty-two..."

He moved forward incrementally, not fast enough.

"Seventy, seventy-one, seventy-two..."

The water splashed into his mouth and he spat it out.

"Eighty, eighty-one, eighty-two..."

Stormy's stroke became weaker and weaker and he wasn't going to reach her.

"Ninety, ninety-one, ninety-two..."

For a moment, I thought I saw Shannon's hand reaching out of the water. Stormy was headed in the wrong direction. I called out, pointed helplessly.

And then I returned to my counting.[7]

---

[7] In Lizzy's initial retelling, it was Stormy who was resting on the long rock while she and Shannon swam and played their breath-holding game. It was during this time that Shannon failed to come up for air. As far as I can tell, Stormy was never interviewed.

The next day, the authorities scoured the lake and recovered Shannon's body. After an autopsy, they ruled the death to be an accidental drowning. But Shannon wasn't a bad swimmer, and I knew the truth.

It was the Lantern Man.[8]

---

[8] Lizzy's therapist, Susan Waugh, theorizes that this was the moment when the story of the Lantern Man shifted from that of mythology into a necessary tool to salvage her own fragile psyche.

Figure 2: "Drowning" by Lizzy Greiner.

OFFICE OF THE MEDICAL EXAMINER
510 Harrison Avenue
Leadville, Colorado 80461

REPORT OF AUTOPSY

DECEDENT: SHANNON GREINER **CASE NUMBER:** ME 2008-000966

MANNER OF DEATH: Accident **IDENTIFIED BY:** Visual

AGE: 16 years
RACE: White
SEX: Female
DATE OF DEATH: Found on July 23, 2007

DATE/TIME OF AUTOPSY: July 27, 2007 @ 9:30 a.m.

PERFORMED BY: Sara H. Zeller, DO, Associate Medical Examiner

CAUSE OF DEATH: Drowning

AUTOPSY FINDINGS

I. Drowning
   A. Witnessed to become submerged in a body of water

II. Blunt and sharp force injuries:
   A. Laceration of left hand, thenar eminence

TOXICOLOGY ANALYSIS: See laboratory report.

CONCLUSION: In consideration of the circumstances surrounding the death, and after examination of the body, it is my opinion that Shannon Greiner, a seventeen-year old female, died as the result of drowning.

Toxicological analysis on tissues obtained at autopsy revealed a small amount of ethyl alcohol, which is due to postmortem bacterial production of alcohol, and is an expected finding with a prolonged postmortem time interval, as in this case.
The manner of death is classified as accident.

Figure 3: Copy of the autopsy summary for Shannon Greiner.

CHAPTER 3

You might have thought that Shannon's body would have been in bad shape after being underwater for so many hours—her flesh and eyes eaten by fish—but it turned out that she was in near pristine condition. I know that because at the funeral they decided on an open casket. I'd never been to a funeral before, much less seen a dead body. And, I won't lie, staring into your own face, post-mortem, is a little disconcerting. There she was, there *I* was, preserved by formaldehyde, mouth sewn shut, makeup slathered over skin. All in all, they did a wonderful job. It's hard to make a dead person look lovely, but they came pretty close.

Not many people came to the funeral because Shannon didn't have many friends. Some teachers came. Some relatives I didn't know we had. It seemed that they were all looking at me, whispering about me behind cupped hands. When I'd make eye contact, they'd purse their lips and shake their heads. Father McBride gave the eulogy, assuring everybody that Shannon was in a better place now, having her soul caressed by Jesus, but his words only succeeded in making me mad and resentful because it all seemed so generic, as if he'd given the speech a dozen times before, instead of being particular to Shannon. Couldn't he have talked about her life, about what made her soul golden? Like how, when she was little, she used to sit cross-legged in the corner of her room and play with her dolls for hours on end, creating a world filled with magic instead of the mean one we lived in? Or how she used to jump from bed to bed all the while singing the lyrics from some masterpiece that she'd created: "I stared at the dead rabbit that I had found; I said the magic words and he hopped to the ground"? Or how, when she got a little older, she'd stare at this photograph of Johnny Depp and have a conversation, promising him that she'd stay true, occasionally leaning in to kiss him (with tongue of course)? What about *her* life, not the life of some place mark soul? Father McBride: "And with a view to eternity, stretching towards heaven, Shannon now rejoices in her perfect union with God himself."

At the burial, the clouds looked like they were ready to burst, but the rain never came. Instead, there was only thunder, sounding like furniture being dragged across the sky. Mom wore a black dress, and her hair was tied in a tight bun. She looked pretty. She couldn't stop crying, though, and her mascara stained her cheeks. Dad and Stormy wore matching black suits that they'd purchased at Goodwill. They both watched stoically, expressions grim, no tears. Their grief wasn't any of my business.

The wind started blowing pretty hard, kicking up dust, and when Father McBride spoke, his words were muffled and hard to hear. At one point, he asked everybody to bow their heads and say a prayer for Shannon, but I couldn't think of anything to say, so I whispered a remembered portion of *Green Eggs and Ham*, just so it looked like I was praying. He asked my father if he wanted to say a few words. Dad shook his head and said, "Let's just get on with things." The priest nodded solemnly and handed him a shovel. Dad dug some dirt from the ground and tossed it into the hole. The moment the soil scattered across the coffin, Stormy released a muffled cry, covering his mouth with his hand. I looked his way and he looked straight back. Now there was only two of us and I knew I'd need Stormy like never before.

I don't want to write about the way my family mourned. I don't want to write about how I became withdrawn and, instead of working hard in class, spent most of my time beneath the bleachers smoking cigarettes and dope. I don't want to write about how my mom, who had once been a very spiritual woman, began praying less and drinking more. And I certainly don't want to write about the steady disintegration of my father.[9]

It used to be that he would come home from the mine every day at five o'clock. He'd kiss Mom on the cheek, ask the kids how our days were, then sit on his recliner and drink beer and watch television, trying, I guess, to numb his mind from the endless hours of soul-crushing work. The life of a working-class man. But after Shannon died, there were some shifts. When he got home, he didn't kiss Mom. He didn't ask Stormy and me how our days were. And now, instead of staring at the television and sucking on his beer, he just sat on that recliner, staring straight ahead, eyes ravaged by impossible pain.

When I talked to him, asked him a question, it seemed that it would take all the energy he could muster just to answer. Several moments would pass and then his head would turn slowly toward

---

[9] Before her sister's death, Lizzy was, by all accounts, a fine student, receiving all As and Bs. She rarely missed class. After the death, Lizzy attended school less and less frequently, and her grades fell rapidly. That is not particularly unusual or surprising for these circumstances. However, her drug use might have some relevance to the investigation. Not only did she smoke marijuana, but her friend, Tabitha Moore, admitted under questioning that the two of them ingested psilocybin mushrooms, MDMA (ecstasy), and Ketamine. Sadly, none of Lizzy's family members seemed willing or capable of helping her through these dark times, as they were also stricken with various levels of grief. There also seems to have been little or no response from the school, although she did meet with a counselor, Theresa Scott, on a single occasion. I spoke with Ms. Scott, and she seemed reticent to reveal their discussions. At first, she claimed privacy laws, but once I informed her that this was a continuation of a criminal investigation, she acquiesced. "She was a strange girl," Ms. Scott told me. "Something wasn't right about her. At one point, she even claimed she was a cold-blooded murderer. When I pressed her on this, she said, 'Not with my hands, but with my thoughts.' She said she would certainly burn in hell for what she had done and what she would do. She quoted a poem by James Wright: 'Wrinkles of winter ditch the rotted face...Dirt of my flesh, defeated, underground.' You want to know the truth? She scared me. I didn't want to ever speak to her again. So I didn't."

me and his lips would part open and he would speak, but his words were jumbled and morbid. Looking back, it seemed that he was dead and gone, just like his daughter, only his body was still tethered to the earth, and he didn't have a knife sharp enough to cut himself away.

He started coming home later and later. Five-thirty. Six. Seven.

And then one night he didn't come home at all.

We ate dinner without him, and there wasn't much conversation, just the sound of silverware clattering against plates. At some point, Stormy asked where Dad was. Mom only shook her head. I think she knew. I think she could sense it.

Stormy and I put dishes away while Mom sat in the living room, sipping on her booze, staring at the dying leaves floating in the glare of the streetlight.

"Wonder where he is," I muttered.

"Don't know."

"Probably went out for a drink."

"Probably."

"Just needed some time on his own."

"Maybe."

The dishes were done. Dad didn't come home. I could tell that Stormy was getting nervous. And Mom hadn't moved from her spot.

Midnight, and I was tired. I didn't want to wait up anymore. I told Stormy goodnight and he hugged me which wasn't like him. When I touched Mom's shoulder, I saw that she was crying, her eyes bloodshot and wounded.

I lay in bed, but I didn't close my eyes. I kept waiting for the sound of the door to open. I heard Mom on the phone, but I couldn't hear what she was saying. Then I saw that the lights were turned off outside my room. I finally closed my eyes.[10]

---

[10] From Detective Kline's notes, it appears that, after leaving his family, Michael drove west (just like he had done after he learned that his wife was pregnant with twins). This time he didn't make it all the way to California, stopping, instead, in Boulder City, Nevada, a small town in the Mojave

Desert. He stayed for several months at the El Rancho Boulder Motel, eventually getting a job as a gas station cashier. He also hooked up with a thrice-divorced woman named Sheila Cartwright, who worked at the same gas station. Detective Kline indicates that after leaving Leadville, Michael didn't call or write his wife or children a single time. While I was unable to contact Mr. Greiner or determine his whereabouts, I was able to connect with Ms. Cartwright over the phone. She described Michael as a funny and smart man who was often quite sweet (bringing her flowers, taking her out to dinner) but also somebody who on a handful of occasions went into a very dark place, which led to heavy drinking and violent outbursts. The most interesting piece of information she revealed was that in the weeks before Lizzy's death, Michael drove back to Leadville on at least three occasions. Both Stormy and Jessica claim that they did not know of Michael's return and that he did not contact either of them.

Figure 4: Clockwise: El Rancho Boulder Motel, the motel where Michael Greiner stayed after leaving behind his family; Boulder City, Nevada postcard; a mugshot of Sheila Cartwright after being arrested for prostitution.

CHAPTER 4

Mother clung hard to her illusions. Despite her daughter's death, despite her husband's abandonment, she never took off her wedding ring, a long-ago promise of love eternal. Did she want to fool the townsfolk or did she want to fool herself? Probably both.

This denial made Stormy angry, I guess. "Does she really think that Dad is going to come back to her? Is that what she thinks? She's a goddamn fool."

And so at some point Stormy came up with a plan. He told me all about it. He'd take the ring off her finger when she was sleeping. Then he'd take it down to the pawn shop and sell it. Use the money to replace one of our windows that had been cracked for a year and a half. The plan made me feel uncomfortable, but I didn't say so. After all, Stormy had his reasons. Then I started thinking about something else. What if Stormy's real motivation to steal the ring was so that he could give it to me? To place it on my finger? The ring was awfully pretty, and that thought made me feel happy.[11]

Of course, it's easier to create a devious plan than to follow through with it. Weeks passed and Stormy didn't do anything about the ring. I thought he'd forgotten about it or maybe chickened out.

But I was wrong.

---

[11] Stormy never planned to sell the ring or give it to Lizzy. He planned to give it to another girl, Nicole McKenna.

It was one of those cold and windy Leadville afternoons, early October, and Stormy and I were just arriving home from school. Actually, I'd pretended to be at school and had actually spent most of the day drawing and writing and smoking cigarettes beneath the bleachers before meeting Stormy and walking home. I knew Mom was home because her car was parked in the driveway and the front door was wide open, the screen door banging open and shut. When we entered the house, I called out, "Mom? Mom?" but there was no answer. I went from room to room, Stormy following me, and was immediately stricken with that old sense of dread. This is what trauma does: it makes you certain that the next trauma is always minutes away. "She might be dead," I said to Stormy, but he only laughed. When we entered the kitchen, I saw that Mom was still alive—no bullet through the temple, no blade through her throat, no poison through her veins.

Instead, she was passed out at the table, something that had been happening with more and more frequency. She was slumped forward in her chair, a wine glass of Southern Comfort shattered on the floor, a lipstick-stained cigarette burning a hole into that week's *People* magazine.[12] Normally, I would have gone and shaken her awake, and she would have mumbled about how she was only drinking because of her insomnia, but this time Stormy stopped me. Instead, he nodded toward her finger, where the ring shone. Then he whispered, "Time's up. I'm gonna get that son-of-a-bitch." While I stood in the entrance of the kitchen, the steady hum of the dishwasher muffling the sound of my own heartbeat, Stormy tiptoed to the sink and squeezed some dish soap onto the palm of his hand and then walked over to where Mom remained slumped. Winking at me, he got to work on slathering the dish soap on the ring finger. Mom didn't move then, and she didn't move when the ring slid easily off. Stormy looked at the glistening rock for a few moments, touched

---

[12] While Jessica admitted to drinking occasionally, she claims that she never drank to excess.

20

it to his mouth, and then placed it in his pocket. Outside I could hear the muffled sound of the church bells.

A short time later, after promising Stormy not to rat him out, I entered my room, the walls covered not with the usual teenage pop idol pictures, but instead with horror movie posters (*The Texas Chainsaw Massacre*, *The Shining*, *The Exorcist*, among others). I went to my desk and flipped through dozens of sketches and drawings of the Lantern Man. I found a blank page and got busy on my latest. The pale face, the gray hair, the empty eyes. In his hand, in addition to a lantern, I drew a pickaxe because I thought there was no tool more fearsome than a pickaxe. And in front of the Lantern Man, a woman who bore more than a slight resemblance to my mother, her head about to be chopped from her torso.

When I was finished with the drawing, one of the best I'd ever done in my humble opinion, I lay on my bed and closed my eyes. Soon I was asleep, dreaming of a world distorted and slanted. Strange creatures appeared and disappeared in my consciousness, whispering sweet and terrifying messages, and I tossed and turned and lashed at the mattress and my pillow. And then another whisper, but this was the voice of my mother.

"Wake up, Lizzy. There's a story I want to tell you."

My eyes flew open. I stared at my mother, her face blurry.

"A story?"

"Yeah. But this one is real. Not like those nightmares your father used to tell you."

"Yes. Okay."

My mother sat down at the edge of the bed. Her face was strained, like a flag. She placed her hands in her lap and, for a few moments, scratched at the skin on her wrist. I thought she would start bleeding, but she didn't. I felt anxious. Soon Mom stopped scratching and stared at the wall behind me. She took a deep breath and then another one. And then she spoke. "When

I was just a girl, probably right around your age, I went out exploring in the woods. It was one of those long, mild summer days like we're bound to have in Leadville. I'd been out for a few hours, just stomping through creeks and grabbing handfuls of flowers, when I spotted this enormous piece of driftwood. It must have washed up from the nearby river. I remember that the wood was gray and twisted and there were small branches jutting out that looked like gnarled fingers. It reminded me of a wise old woman somehow, and I figured it would be perfect to take home and paint, make into my own piece of art. You probably don't know this, but I used to be a creative type. Had one of my paintings in the high school art show. The driftwood was heavy though, and I was forced to drag it through the forests and hills, the way a murderer might drag a corpse." My mother paused, a faint smile visible on her face. "Anyway, by the time I finally got it home, maybe an hour later, the skin on my hands and wrists was torn and blistered and I was exhausted. I managed to sneak the driftwood into my room—I knew my mother would make me leave nature where it belonged—and for the next several days I worked hours on end creating the most amazing piece of art, splattered with purples and oranges and blues and yellows.

"But things are never what they seem, Lizzy. You see, I had only just finished painting the driftwood, when I noticed that the colors were beginning to change, the wood beginning to split. And then, upon closer inspection, I saw something moving. I looked closer. It was a large red ant. I blinked a few times, but it was no good. I saw another one and another one. Well, it didn't take me long to realize that my precious piece of driftwood had been infested by carpenter ants and that soon they would burrow tunnels. I'd worked hard on that piece of art, but I had no choice but to take the wood into the fire pit outside and light a match to it. It lit fast and was quickly consumed. That should have been the end of it. But what I didn't know, Lizzy, is that the ants had already burrowed into the floor and furniture. What I didn't know is that they would soon infest damn near our entire house. My poor old dad, your grandfather, was forced to pull up all the floorboards with a claw hammer. Then he dumped boric acid on the goddamn ants. There must have been a thousand of them."

I waited for the rest of the story, but that was it. There was nothing more to be said. "It's too bad," I finally said. "I bet the driftwood would have been pretty."

Mom sighed deeply. "Yes. Too bad. So we learn," and now she glared at me, "best not to infest your own house."

I looked away. "I suppose you're right."

Out of the corner of my eyes, I could see my mother looking down at her hands again, bare of her engagement ring. More anxiety. Then she leaned toward me, and I could feel her breath on my cheeks. When she spoke again, her voice was full of rasp.

"Your daddy gave me that ring," she said, "on the day he asked me to marry him."

"What...what are you talking about?"

"Don't play dumb, girl. Best to wait until I'm dead to take it off my finger."

"I didn't—"

Then she smiled bitterly, her eyes rolling back into her skull, and I knew she was thinking about him and wishing he was here to hold her, here to keep her warm from the mountain winds, here to keep her company on those lonely nights. And maybe she was thinking of Shannon, too, her angel taken away as a test of her eternal faith, a female Job. At that moment I wanted to kiss her on the cheek because I realized she was a good woman who'd been wronged by this mean old world. But before I could lean forward, my mother's eyes fluttered open, and she nodded briskly at me.

"Now. Lizzy. I'll say it once. Give me the ring back."

"I...I don't have the ring."

Her face began to redden. "Yes, you do. You took it while I was sleeping. I know that now."

"No, ma'am."

And now a slap to the cheek. And then another one. Harder.

"Don't lie to me, girl. Give me back the ring."

"I don't have it." And right then, though I could have cut my losses and ratted Stormy out, I made up my mind that I would never tell her that he'd stolen the ring, no matter what.

My mother's shoulders were rising up and down and her left eye was twitching. I wondered what my punishment would be. Would she burn me with a cigarette? Hold my head under the bathwater? Tear out of a clump of my hair?

She raised her hand like she was going to strike again, but this time she dropped her fist back to her lap. She took a few deep breaths and said, "Okay, Lizzy. That's just fine."

I eyed Mom suspiciously. "What's fine?"

"Everything. Everything's fine. But what I'd like you to do is to go outside and spend some time in the Chevy."

"The Chevy?"

"Yes. I want you to sit there thinking about what you done, thinking about what it means to be a Christian."

I nodded my head. "Yes, ma'am. How long you want me to sit?"

"I guess until you're ready to give me back my ring."

"I never took your ring, Mom. Honestly, I didn't."

But she wouldn't listen to me. Eventually I gave in.

And so I sat there in the truck for four hours, five hours, six, all the while shivering in the cold. The whole time I sang Elvis Presley songs and told myself princess stories. Not typical princess stories where she overcomes the evil witch and settles down with a handsome prince, but ones where she meets a horrendous fate like burning to death in a witch's oven because that's more entertaining for everybody involved.[13]

---

[13] While Jessica Greiner never got her ring back, Stormy denied stealing it from her. And, sad to say, Lizzy did eventually meet that horrendous fate in a witch's oven.

Figure 5: "Mother" by Lizzy Greiner.

CHAPTER 5

The next several weeks were a miserable blur. Sometimes I went to school. Other times I skipped and went exploring through the streets and hills of Leadville, the old mountain mining town where I've lived my whole life. According to Ms. Fisher (my obese history teacher), the gold rush took place here more than one-hundred-fifty years ago. They discovered millions of dollars' worth of gold using sluice and pan. And once the gold ran out, silver was up next. That's what really made this town great. They all moved here to strike it rich, and in the meantime, they built hotels and saloons and brothels. The prostitutes and drunks are still here, but most of the rest are gone. The way Stormy tells it, Leadville is like a woman. Once she was beautiful and covered with silver and everybody wanted a piece, but then she got old and dried up, so they left her to die alone.

During those weeks, Mom never mentioned the ring, even though she obviously suspected that I had it. In fact, for the most part, she stopped talking to me completely, focusing instead on work (Tennessee Pass Café) and booze (Southern Comfort). So most of the time it was just me and Stormy, and that was okay. That was how it was supposed to be.

But then Stormy met a girl and everything changed.[14]

Truth be told, Nicole McKenna was probably the prettiest

---

[14] Nicole and Stormy started dating in early October, four months after Shannon's death, and one month after Michael left the family.

girl at Lake County High School. She had long hair piled into a swirl of gold and always seemed to be smiling, her teeth white and straight behind candy-cherry red lips. She wasn't a cheerleader and wasn't homecoming queen, but she probably should have been. And unlike most of the other so-called popular girls in school, people actually liked her. She'd talk to you and laugh at your jokes and help you with homework. So it made sense that Stormy started dating her. Because he was the only one good enough for her.

And maybe it was understandable that I felt a bit jealous when I first saw Stormy talking and laughing with Nicole in front of his locker. She was holding her books against her chest and twirling her hair—so obviously pleased to have finally gained his full attention. He was leaning forward, his triceps muscle purposefully twitching. Maybe they're just friends, I thought, but I knew right away that I was lying to myself, like I was bound to do. I'd lost my sister. I'd lost my father. I couldn't afford to lose Stormy, too.

Watching them over the next several weeks was sickening. You can imagine. Everywhere Stormy went, Nicole went. In between classes they would hold hands and laugh and be happier than anybody had the right to be—especially in school. Whenever I saw them, I pretended not to notice, staring, instead, at the floor beneath me or the classroom ahead of me. But one day, Stormy spotted me rushing down the hallway to my Spanish class and called out, "Hey, Squirt, where's the fire?" I had no choice. I was forced to stop and turn. I smiled sheepishly. Stormy and Nicole. Nicole and Stormy. Ah, hell.

But still, I flashed a crooked smile, trying to look like I didn't have a care in the world. What me worry, bitches? "Oh, hey, Stormy. Didn't see you there."

A moment's indecision, and then Stormy said, "You know Nicole? Her brother's in some of your classes, I think. Bobby's his name."[15]

"I know Bobby," I said, even though I didn't.

"Nice to meet you, Lizzy," Nicole said, sticking out her slender hand, the nails painted and perfectly manicured. "I've heard a lot about you."

Heard a lot about me? What the hell was that supposed to mean? What had Stormy told her? About how I went to bed with my tennis shoes on, just in case I had to escape in the middle of the night? About how I chewed my fingernails *and* toenails completely off because of my anxiety? About what an all-around freak I was? And where had he found the time to tell these things to her? Certainly not in class. Where then? On romantic walks by the creek? At Nicole's house while her parents were at work?

A few questions to think about: Did she stick her tongue down his throat? Did she take off her shirt and show him her pretty little titties? Did she maneuver her hand down his pants and grasp his swollen cock? Did she let him place it in her lipsticked mouth?[16]

"Nice to meet you, too," I said. And, once again, I smiled my nicest smile.

An awkward pause, and then my brother said, "Say, sis, do you mind walking home on your own today? Me and Nicole are going to study a bit. For our trig test. It's gonna be a beast. Sine and cosine. Makes no sense whatsoever. But Nicole's twice as smart as me. And you gotta use the help when you can get it."

I nodded my head, trying to be agreeable. "Yeah, no problem. I can walk alone." Then, trying not to sound desperate: "What time will you be home, do you think?"

"Not sure." He winked. "But don't wait up for me."

For just a moment I hated my brother.

---

[15] Of Lizzy, Bobby McKenna said, "She was crazy. That's what everybody said. We only spoke once, but she scared me. Out of nowhere, she told me that God was hanging from a noose. Told me the devil had made it look like suicide. I had no fucking idea what she was talking about. Yeah, she scared me. But she really scared my sister."

[16] Nicole claims that she and Stormy never had sexual relations.

"Okay," I said before returning my gaze to Nicole. "I hope you guys have fun." *Stupid whore.*

"Thanks, Lizzy! I'll be seeing you around, I'm sure."

"Yeah, okay."

And as I continued to my Spanish class (yes, I was going to class today), it took all the willpower I could muster to prevent myself from breaking down into tears right there in the hallway. Because Stormy liked another girl. Because I wasn't so special anymore.

All through class, I couldn't focus on anything except for Stormy and Nicole. I doodled hateful images and was sulky and sassy when the teacher called on me. I knew I was acting like a child, but maybe that's because I *was* a child. Think about it. I'd never had a real boyfriend, never even kissed a boy. I was as flat as an ironing board. Couldn't even drive a car. Yes, that was it. I was just a girl. And I supposed there was nothing to do about these jealous and angry feelings except allow them to fester. Or to act on them. Split the whore's face like a grape. Great options, both.[17]

But after school, I didn't walk home by myself like I'd promised Stormy I would. Instead, I did my best to blend into the teenage crowd that rushed through the doors, and then squatted behind a bush until I spotted Stormy and Nicole, the two lovebirds. They were holding hands, which was bad enough, but then, as I skulked behind them, I saw Stormy lean over and kiss her on

---

[17] During the weeks that followed, Lizzy focused most of her rage toward Nicole, not her brother. Detective Kline recovered several letters that she wrote, addressed to Nicole, never sent. Most of them were violent in nature, promising to do things like "use a knife to slit a crooked grin onto your throat" and to "turn your skin into a throw rug in the living room." Other times, the letters were more conciliatory. For example, she wrote, "Wouldn't it be great if we became sisters? I'd be honored to have someone as gorgeous and smart and kind in my family." Despite the disturbing nature of many of the recovered letters, there is no indication that she ever harmed Nicole.

the lips. I wanted to scream, to howl at the sky, but instead I just kept following them and I didn't know why.

They left the school grounds and walked slowly into the nearby neighborhoods filled with old converted mining cabins and Victorian houses—some of them well-maintained, most of them rotting into the dirt. Dogs barked and trees trembled in the breeze. I wasn't far behind them—no more than twenty yards. If they looked back and saw me, I'd say that I'd lost my house key and needed to borrow his. But they were only focused on each other, and so they never did look back, not a single time.[18]

Nicole lived in one of the bigger houses in the neighborhood, a pretty blue Victorian protected by a white picket fence. Still holding hands and now laughing (why did laughter always feel so exclusionary?), Stormy and Nicole walked through the gate, up the steps, and into the house. Stormy closed the door behind them. I stood across the street, still as a sniper, the wind blowing, dead leaves scattering. Remember when Stormy loved me? Remember? Like when I had fallen from a pine tree and broken my left wrist, the bone jutting through my skin, he'd been the one who'd carried me in his arms—just like a princess—a mile and a half down the hill to our house. Or when I'd been bullied by the fat kid with the piggy nose; he'd been the one who'd found the kid at school, slammed him against the wall, and told him to never, ever say an unkind word to his sister again. Yes, he used to love me. Don't you think? I remained motionless for a long time, just staring at the house, and I wished to God that the world was less mean and less lonely. Eventually, my legs became tired, and so I walked down a dirt alley, sat against an

---

[18] This was not the only time Lizzy followed Stormy and Nicole home. In fact, according to Nicole, Lizzy followed them every single day for several weeks. She would sit cross-legged across the street and watch the house, making no real effort to conceal her presence. Stormy assured Nicole that it was just a phase that Lizzy was going through and there was nothing to be alarmed about. Sympathetic, Nicole agreed not to tell her parents. For a long time, Mr. and Mrs. McKenna did not even know that Stormy had a sister. Not until they found her sleeping, uninvited, in Nicole's bed.

old wooden shed, and rested my chin on my knees. Up ahead, the Rocky Mountains loomed tall and dark, and I squeezed my eyes shut, thinking about violence and redemption, Christ and the devil. Those types of things.

I must have fallen asleep because when I opened my eyes, my body jerked and it was dark and I didn't know where I was. A streetlight flickered on, and I saw that there was a figure standing over me, face hidden by shadows.

I gasped, thinking it was the Lantern Man[19], but then the figure bent down and I realized that it was my brother. My skull was stuffed full with misery and I started crying and crying; I just couldn't help myself.

Stormy sat down next to me and smoothed back my hair and shushed me and said, "It's okay, Squirt. There's no need to cry. I'm right here."

Another few minutes of sobbing and then I stopped, wiping my eyes with the sleeve of my shirt. "I'm sorry," I said. "I shouldn't have come here. I only missed you is all. I should have gone home."

He smiled and it was a smile of kindness and goodness. "You don't have to be sorry, kiddo. I shouldn't have left you alone like that. I was only thinking about me. C'mon. Get to your feet. Let's walk home. Mom is probably worried sick."

"Mom doesn't care."

"Ah, you know that's not true."

"Maybe not. But I like saying it because I like feeling sorry for myself."

"Yeah, I guess you do."

Overhead the moon was the color of bone. Off in the distance, a pair of dogs were barking, and they wouldn't shut up. I would have felt scared but not with my brother here. He reached out a hand and pulled me to my feet. I shivered—the wind was blowing—and so he pulled off his leather jacket and placed it around

---

[19] By this point, she had already become consumed with the Lantern Man (notebooks filled with drawings and stories).

my shoulders.

We walked through the alley and toward Harrison Street, lined with old brick buildings, many of them with faded advertisements on the side. The cars had turned their headlights on. For several blocks, neither one of us spoke. Down Third Street and a left on Leiter, and we came to our house, a little shotgun shack that had once been used as storage for the Conger Mine.

Stormy squeezed my shoulder. "There's something you should know," he said. "She doesn't mean much to me."

"Who?"

"That girl. Nicole. She's nice, but she's just a girl. You don't have to worry about her. I promise that you'll always be my number one."

And I smiled because Stormy had never broken a promise before.[20]

---

[20] Dr. Waugh felt that Lizzy's possessiveness of her brother reached a pathological level. The trauma of losing both her sister and father likely contributed to this pathology. Dr. Waugh called this neurosis a "modified version of the Electra Complex." In Jungian psychology, the Electra Complex occurs when a girl has a psychosexual competition with her mother over the love of her father. In Lizzy's case, however, she was competing with Nicole for the love of her brother.

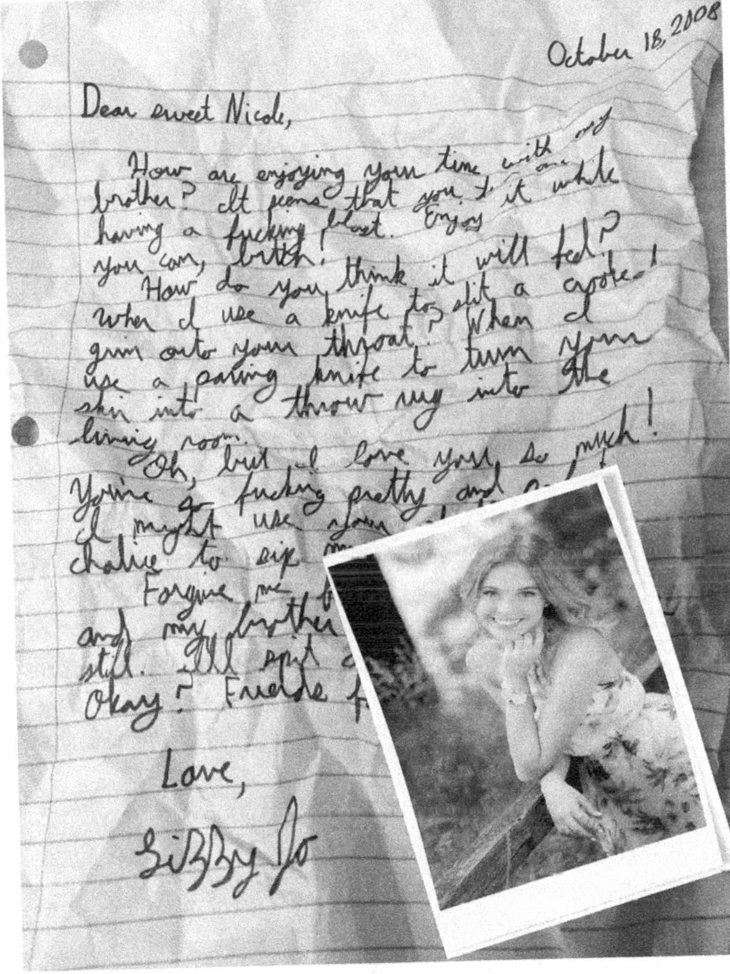

October 18, 2008

Dear sweet Nicole,

How are enjoying your time with my brother? It seems that you & it are while having a fucking blast. Enjoy you can, bitch!

How do you think it will feel when I use a knife to slit a crooked grin onto your throat? When I use a paring knife to turn your skin into a throw rug into the living room.

Oh, but I love you so much! You're so fucking pretty and ... I might use your ... chalice to sip ...

Forgive me, ... and my brother ... still. I'll spit ... Okay? Freddie f...

Love,

Lizzy Jo

Figure 6: One of the letters that Lizzy wrote to Nicole but never sent. On top of the letter is Nicole's senior picture.

CHAPTER 6

But it didn't take long for me to realize that Stormy *had* broken his promise, that I was no longer his number one. Now Stormy and Nicole walked home together every day. Now I was forced to eat dinner alone or with my mother each night. She and I barely talked, of course. But I knew what she was thinking. *Where's my ring, you little whore? Is it up your snatch? Is that where it is?*

In the dark and quiet of my room I would think of my brother and Nicole, together, alone, and I would feel sick to my stomach, feel like I wanted to scream. It was in those terribly lonely moments that I would recall the story of Leadville's own Baby Doe, the poor but lovely lady who had seduced and eventually married the silver tycoon, Horace Tabor. Rags to riches. Happily ever after. But no, that wasn't real life. You see, Horace, once the richest man in all of Colorado, was stupid and prideful, as men tend to be, and he lost it all in just a few months. Legend has it that near the end of his life he was shoveling slag from Cripple Creek mines for three bucks a day, telling anybody who would listen that his famous Matchless Mine would produce again and make Baby Doe rich. But it never happened and poor Baby Doe spent the rest of her days destitute, once again, in a tiny shack right behind the mine. She barely ever left, except when she was in need of food. Then she'd go sneaking into town, a skeleton of a woman dressed in rags, barely recognizable from her celebrity status of days gone by. And sometimes she'd steal food and sometimes she'd beg, and then she'd once again disappear into her shack not to be seen for some months. A neighbor watched out for the old woman, but one day when she didn't see smoke coming from the chimney of the shack, she went inside and found Baby Doe frozen to death, stretched out stiff on the floor.

Is there any story sadder that? Anything lonelier? But what do you do with loneliness? What do you do with sadness? Better to hurt, I decided, than to be hurt.[21]

The girl's name was Sierra Bowden. She was a tall wanna-be hooker who wore several coats of makeup and bathed in cheap perfume. Her most impressive feature was located just below her collar bone; what I mean by that is if she jumped on a trampoline, she'd probably give herself a pair of black eyes. Anyway, Tabitha Moore, the anorexic cutter and my only real friend, told me that Sierra was spreading rumors about me. Nasty ones. About all the boys that I'd blown (when, in fact, it had been a grand total of zero). About my lack of hygiene (according to her, I didn't ever trim my bush). About how I wanted to do my own brother. In the past, I might have ignored the nastiness. In the past, I might have laughed it off. And in the past, Stormy would have stood up for me. He would have approached the dumb bitch, stuck his finger into her face, and said, "Stop talking shit about my sister. You hear me? Stop talking shit."

But Stormy wasn't focused on protecting his sister anymore. Stormy was only focused on the sweet promises of newfound

---

[21] Dr. Waugh told me that Lizzy was fascinated with Baby Doe, as well as the authors Virginia Woolf and Sylvia Plath, and talked about them frequently. Interestingly, all three of these women died in particularly cruel ways—Doe by the aforementioned freezing, Woolf by drowning (she weighed down her pockets with stones and walked into a river), and Plath by carbon monoxide poisoning (she placed her head in a gas oven and sealed the room shut).

love—kisses in the rain, flesh against flesh, whispers in the moonlight (blah, blah, blah). I'd rather shave my head with a cheese grater, I decided, than enter into that world of sickening tenderness.

So instead of waiting for my fraternal savior, I took matters into my own hands. On this particular morning, I was walking down the hallway, humming Johnny Cash's "Ring of Fire," when I saw Sierra and her group of bimbo friends congregating around the lockers, certainly discussing important subjects like homecoming dresses and tampons and mascara. When they spotted me, Sierra nodded and laughed and then muttered some snide remarks to her crew. And they all laughed with her because there is nothing more amusing than being superior to somebody else.

Understand that I wasn't a violent person by nature, but because of my sister's death and my father's abandonment, I had become an angry one. I stopped in my tracks and glared at Sierra, her tanned cleavage welcoming the stares of every male horn-dog in school. My breath quickened and my fists tightened. No hesitation as I dropped my backpack to the floor and strode straight toward the brothel-in-making. A few of the girls backed up or moved to the side, but Sierra held her ground, the queen bee. "What do you want, freak?" she said, and that was enough.[22]

I charged forward, fists swinging wildly, connecting several times to the jaw and temple before Sierra had a chance to react. She was no fighter, that quickly became obvious. Instead of kicking or punching back, she went into full defensive mode, covering her face with her hands. The last thing she needed was to have a fat lip or black eye for the homecoming dance, the biggest and most crucial night of her life.

She would soon have both.

It seemed that it was only a matter of seconds before half the school was surrounding the main event. I had Missy Bimbo on

---

[22] Sierra claimed that she never laughed at Lizzy, and that, until the fight, she didn't even know who Lizzy was. She also denied ever calling her a "freak." I did not interview other students on this matter.

the ground and was pulling back her hands so I could better punish her face. I scratched, I hit, I bit. The other students watched in horror/amusement as Sierra's face became less and less pretty (not that she had ever been a natural beauty). Her friends avoided intervention—partly because they didn't want their own lipstick to get smeared and partly because they too thought Sierra had it coming.

It seemed like I was pummeling her for a long time, but it was probably less than two minutes before a few teachers got wind of the fight and dove in to break it up. Mrs. Samuelson, the librarian with the goiter, got behind me and tried pulling me off. But I was smart and grabbed at Sierra's beautiful bleached hair. As the teacher pulled me away, I tugged hard and managed to yank out damn near her entire ponytail. With a rebel's yell, I victoriously held it high in the air like some war trophy.[23]

Once they finally got me into the office, Mr. Jenkins, the height-challenged principal, pointed his teeny-weeny finger into my face and said, "How dare you?" not once, not twice, but three times. And now I wanted to get into another fight, just because. But I held back on punching Mr. Jenkins because expulsion wasn't what I needed. Not yet, anyway.

He placed me in a chair in his office and I screamed again. "You calm the hell down," he said in his tough-guy voice and then left, slamming the door behind him. I slumped down in the chair, and I thought about my dead sister. I thought about Stormy and the ring. Through the window I could see the principal and his harem of secretaries, watching guardedly, the way they might watch a rabid squirrel.

After some time, Mr. Jenkins poked his head in the office

---

[23] Sierra went to the hospital and was treated for a ruptured eardrum, a bloodied face and scalp, and a black eye. The next day, her mother, Gwendy Bowden, threatened to sue the school for lack of supervision, but she soon backed off. Sierra returned to school three days later and is now fully recovered.

and said, "Your mother is on her way. We've apprised her of the situation." Then he closed the door, perhaps petrified, just a bit, by me, a girl psychopath.

Sixth period passed and then seventh, and nobody spoke to me. That was just fine. A moral lecture wasn't what I was looking for. Finally, I saw my mother standing in front of the doorway, chatting with Mr. Jenkins, nodding her head every half second or so. She wore blue jeans and a red and black flannel shirt and her hair was a mess and so was her face. I felt embarrassed. A woman who drank before noon. Who spent her life serving slop at the local diner. Who would almost certainly die alone. Just like Baby Doe.

The two of them entered, and Mr. Jenkins was now smiling stiffly, but not my mother. She looked petrified, unsure of her role. *To be a mother,* I thought. *To stand up for me.*

"As you might imagine," the little guy said, "Sierra's parents are very upset. She's probably going to need to get stitches on her scalp. It's hard to know exactly what the fight started over. It's possible that Sierra said something to Lizzy. That's the way these things usually go. Lizzy? Did she say something to you?"

I didn't respond, just remained staring straight ahead.

"In any case, Lizzy went after her. Got in some good shots. Yanked out a chunk of her hair."

And that was all he said for a while. An awkward silence as he glanced at me and then at my mother and then back at me again.

Again, the little man: "Of course, we want what's best for Lizzy, too. We don't simply want to act punitively. I know you've all been dealing with a lot in your personal lives. A question for you. Has she been acting out like this at home? Showing fits of violence?"

Mom opened her mouth as if to speak but then closed it again. What was she, a fucking mute?

"I think what would be best," said Mr. Jenkins, "is if we suspended her for five days. That's the maximum allowed by the district. That would give her a chance to think about her actions. And it would send the right message to everybody involved. What do you think, Mrs. Greiner?"

Think about my actions. What a bunch of bullshit. Well, at least I wouldn't have to sit in the car this time.

And now, the mute spoke. "Okay, Mr. Jenkins," she said. "I think that's fair. I think I'll take her home now, if that's okay."

Mr. Jenkins nodded and patted my shoulder. Now started the act that always happened when parents were present. "I know a couple of secrets about you," he said, not unkindly. "I know you're a smart girl. I know you're a kind girl. Even if you don't always act like it."

I narrowed my eyes, and a little grin spread across my face. "She had such pretty hair, mister. But I tore that shit out."[24]

---

[24] The principal, Don Jenkins, didn't know Lizzy well. Until she began missing classes and getting into fights, she hadn't been sent to his office a single time. However, I learned that Stormy had been disciplined several times over the past two years: twice for fighting, once for cheating, and once for bullying. Mr. Jenkins played off most of these incidents with a shrug and a "boys will be boys" attitude, but he did mention that, during his sophomore year, Stormy had been suspended for "slut shaming" a girl named ███. Once the incident was reported, Stormy was very contrite, and later, under administration pressure, wrote a letter apologizing for his "disgraceful behavior." See figure 7 for a copy of the letter. When I first read the letter, I thought that it was respectful and heartfelt. But then I looked closer and noticed that the first letter on each line (after the greeting) creates a message, and then I realized that he hadn't been sorry at all.

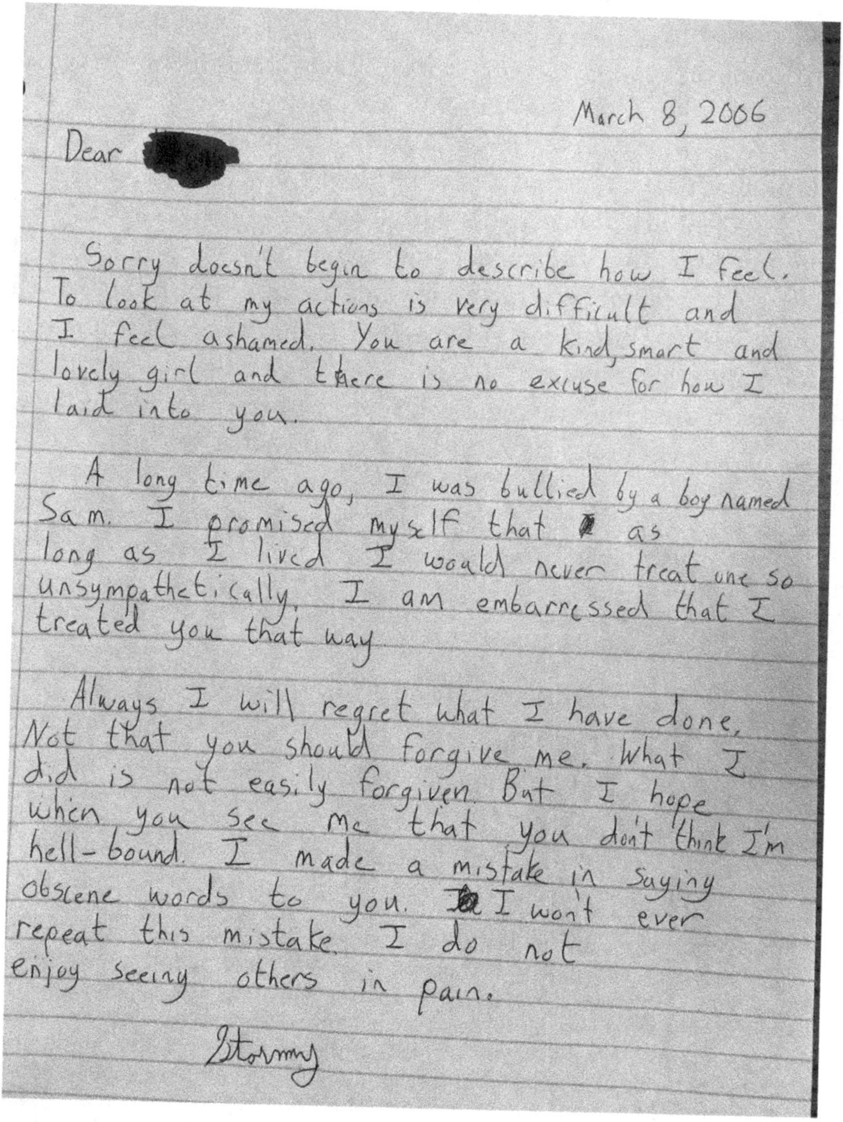

March 8, 2006

Dear ████

Sorry doesn't begin to describe how I feel. To look at my actions is very difficult and I feel ashamed. You are a kind, smart and lovely girl and there is no excuse for how I laid into you.

A long time ago, I was bullied by a boy named Sam. I promised myself that I as long as I lived I would never treat one so unsympathetically. I am embarrassed that I treated you that way.

Always I will regret what I have done. Not that you should forgive me. What I did is not easily forgiven. But I hope when you see me that you don't think I'm hell-bound. I made a mistake in saying obscene words to you. I won't ever repeat this mistake. I do not enjoy seeing others in pain.

Stormy

Figure 7: Stormy's apology letter.

CHAPTER 7

The next several days were actually pretty damn relaxing. I ate a lot and smoked a lot and slept a lot and drew a lot. Stormy gave me a hard time about the fight. "Pulling hair?" he said. "That's not like you. That's so...girly." I laughed because there was no bigger putdown from Stormy than being girly. Most of the time, though, even after school, he wasn't around. He was with Nicole. And if I were really being honest with myself, it was Nicole whose ponytail I wanted to rip out.

During the day, it wasn't so bad because I knew they were in class, but at night I hurt and felt jealous. Sometimes the pain was such that I would steal a taste of my mother's Southern Comfort (God's nastiest creation), sneak out of the house, and ride my bike to Nicole's house where the two of them were likely sitting on her bed "studying." I would stare at that upstairs window, light glowing behind a white curtain, and torture myself by imagining what they were really doing, always something naughty, always something sordid. I don't know why I cared so much. After all, he was a young man, and he was free to do as he pleased. Why did it matter if he had a crush on Nicole? Who wouldn't have a crush on Nicole? Why did it matter that they spent time together? Why did it bother me that he was so damn happy? Well. It was because I felt excluded. That's what it was.

And when one feels excluded, when one feels disconnected, sometimes bad things happen.[25]

Yes, I watched that house. I watched that window. I wondered what Nicole's family was like. I wondered what the inside of the house was like. Perfect, probably, both.[26] And then there was this: on two separate occasions, I'd seen where Nicole hid her key—beneath a flower pot at the edge of her porch.

I knew that if I thought about something for a long enough time, eventually I'd do it. So there I was, on the fourth day of my suspension, standing across the street from the house, staring at that flower pot, thinking, thinking. And they were dark thoughts, despite the sun shining overhead in that beautiful blank sky. A mailman walked down the sidewalk, whistling, but he never noticed me. I'd never been very noticeable—a blessing and a curse. I took a deep breath and then smiled, feigning confidence, before walking across the street, all quiet and still. Moments later, I was fumbling with the latch, every now and then glancing behind me for any signs of life. I finally managed to open the gate and then strode toward the front porch, toward the flower pot. *Just act like you live here and nobody will care,* and it was probably true. With a spurt of courage, I tipped back the flower pot and snatched the key, the rusted metal scraping against the porch cement. I studied that key for a long moment, whispered a prayer to nobody, and walked up the steps toward the front door. With trembling hands, I jiggled the key in the keyhole and

---

[25] On the evening of October 22nd, a neighbor of Nicole's called the police to report a girl "acting awfully strange." The neighbor said that the girl was waving her arms like they were wings and alternating between sobbing loudly and laughing maniacally. At one point, she got to her knees and began pulling out plants and flowers and eating them. The police eventually arrived at the scene, but the girl had left. It is possible this girl was Lizzy.

[26] On numerous occasions, Lizzy told Dr. Waugh that Nicole was a "perfect girl" and "probably didn't have a single problem in this world." However, Nicole suffered from a severe eating disorder (bulimia), and her parents were in the process of divorcing.

shouldered open the door. Then I stepped inside and this was where Nicole lived. Holy shit, this was where Nicole lived.

The inside of the house was pretty and tidy. *Just like Nicole.* Nature photographs hung from the wall: moose and snow and mountains. There was a couch and a coffee table and a television. There were also bookshelves lined with books. Home decoration and self-help and photography.

I wandered into the kitchen and opened the refrigerator. It was filled with breads and meats and cheeses and fruits and vegetables. All the wholesome foods that made Nicole such a wholesome girl. Ah, what the hell. I could be wholesome, too. I found an overly ripe plum and washed it in the sink. I took a bite and the red juice spilled down my chin. I took another bite and another, not bothering to wipe the juice from my face. Then I tossed the pit in the trash and continued roaming through the house. Hallway, dining room, bathroom. They never fought in this house, I figured. The only tears were those of joy. I came to the wooden staircase and slowly ascended. An antique mirror hung from the wall and I grinned, the red juice on my chin looking suspiciously like blood.

Atop the stairs, family portraits hung from the wall, and in every one they were happy, thrilled really, smiles so wide as to cause aneurysms. Nicole's mother looked just like her daughter, a fresh-faced blonde with perfect bone structure. Certainly, many years back, she'd been prom queen in some small Ohio town[27] and had refused to let her date touch her boobs because she wasn't that kind of a girl. Nicole's father wore khakis and a polo shirt. He must have been an insurance salesman or a Realtor or a golf pro.[28] Her brother also wore a polo shirt, and soon he would help run his old man's business.[29]

I walked down the hallway, peeking inside each room. A

---

[27] She actually grew up in Denver. I didn't investigate whether she had been prom queen.

[28] He worked at the bank and was recently laid off.

[29] Bobby McKenna: "I just want to get the hell out of this goddamn town and away from my goddamn father."

study with an old walnut desk and a leather chair. A master bedroom with a king-sized bed, a rocking chair, and a sturdy dresser. Her brother's room, with basketballs and baseballs and gloves and sports posters. And finally, to Nicole's room. Oh, what a pleasure! The walls were pink...just because. And hanging from the walls were posters of teen heart throbs (Josh Hartnett, Zac Efron, Orlando Bloom) as well as photo collages of all her pretty friends from school, and they were all laughing, hugging, and having a great fucking time. On top of each collage, written in glitter pen, were phrases like "Friends Forever!" and "Fun in the Sun!" There was a volleyball signed by each girl on the high school team and a Cinderella-style dress that she would wear to Homecoming. On her bed were a dozen fluffy purple and pink pillows, as well as several stuffed animals (how cute was the little teddy bear!). I laughed in spite of myself because Nicole's room was exactly the way I'd imagined it. So this was the girl Stormy had chosen! Barf, barf, barf. If Stormy had picked some tough girl with Joan Jett hair and a leather jacket, I wouldn't have been bothered. If he'd picked some mousy, nose-in-a-book girl, I wouldn't have been bothered, either. But Nicole. *She* bothered me.

It must be nice, I thought, to have such a happy family, to always be smiling and to have fluffy pillows and stuffed animals and collages that said "Fun in the Sun." It must be nice not to have a sister who drowned and a father who split and a mother who drank before noon. It must be nice not to be suspended for yanking a ponytail out of some girl's scalp.

I strode across the room toward Nicole's dresser. I opened a few drawers until I found some undergarments. Soft panties. Expensive bras. I grabbed a pair of white panties and touched them to my face, sniffed. Then I stuffed them in my pocket. I don't know why.[30]

---

[30] Nicole's panties weren't the only thing Lizzy stole. Investigators found several of Nicole's necklaces, a pair of earrings, and a half-dozen family photographs.

Over the next couple of days, I spent a lot of time inside Nicole's house. Don't judge! I ate her food. I watched her TV. I listened to her stereo. I even pooped in her toilet once. It was all in good fun and I figured I could get used to this.

Maybe it was the turkey sandwich I'd eaten or the Busch beer I'd drunk, but on this particular afternoon I felt exhausted. I hadn't been sleeping well, not while wearing my tennis shoes, always ready to run. I could take a little nap now. Yes, just lie down on Nicole's beautiful bed and squeeze tight that cute little teddy bear. It was, what, one o'clock? Nobody would be home for a while, not for a couple of hours anyway. Just a little nap. I stretched out my body, yawned, and lay on the bed. At first, I remained above the covers because I didn't want to have to remake the bed, but the promise of slumber was so enticing, and I was so tired, that I gave into the temptation, pulling back the covers and snuggling in underneath. I felt safe lying there, smelling the sweet scent of Nicole's perfume and moisturizers, imagining that my own father was an insurance salesman with a polo shirt and my own mother had beautiful blue eyes and wasn't a drunk. Imagining, in fact, that I *was* Nicole. *And in next to no time, Goldilocks lay fast asleep in Baby Bear's bed.*

For the first time in a long time, I slept deeply and without anxiety. For the first time in a long time, I had no nightmares. But deep sleep had its own problems as the clock moved from two o'clock, then three o'clock, then four o'clock. Sweet dreams, and I didn't hear the front door bang open. Didn't hear a woman's voice call out, "Nicole? Are you home?" Didn't hear the footsteps echoing in the hallway. Didn't hear the bedroom door creak open and the woman gasp in surprise.

"Oh, Lord Jesus," she said. "Who the hell are you? What are you doing here? I'll call the cops."

My eyes flew open and I quickly pulled myself up in the bed.

The woman from the photos, the woman who was once a prom queen in a small town in Ohio, stood over me, a puzzled expression on her face.

"What are you doing in Nicole's bed? What—"

"I...I'm a friend," I said. "My name's Lizzy. Stormy's my brother."

"Stormy?"

"Yes. Nicole's boyfriend."

"You mean Brandon?"

"Yes. I call him Stormy. I always have."

And now I was out of the bed, trying, in a panic, to remake the covers. Mrs. McKenna, Nicole's mother, remained where she was, hands on her hips, scowl on her face.

"I'm very sorry," I said. "I was just so tired, and...I'll be going now. It was a mistake."

But I'd only taken a single step forward when Stormy and Nicole appeared in the doorframe, hand in hand.

Up until that point, I don't recall Stormy ever shouting at me. Not a single time. Not when, at age eight, I used his baseball cards to start a bonfire. Not when, at age ten, I used his school book report to make a paper airplane. Not when, at age thirteen, I barged into his room while he was...pleasuring himself. And in the moments following the discovery in Nicole's room, Stormy didn't shout at me then either. Instead, he took a deep breath, shook his head, and apologized profusely to both Nicole and Mrs. McKenna. "Things have been tough on her lately," he said. "Not to make excuses, but I'm sure she didn't mean any harm. Girls do silly things sometimes." Eventually they accepted the apology, but both eyed me with disdain and fear (thoughts of Lizzy Borden instead of Lizzy Greiner, perhaps?). When there was nothing left to say, when it was obvious that Nicole and Mrs. McKenna just wanted me to be gone, Stormy, with maybe a bit more force than necessary, grabbed me by the hand and led me the hell out of that place. I ruin everything I do.

As we walked home, Stormy didn't say a word. I talked a lot, trying to explain what had happened, promising that it would never happen again. "I've missed you so much, Stormy, and it seems as if Nicole is just getting in the way, leaving me sad and sometimes lonely..." Stormy kept his head down, stewing. Still, no shouting.

But when we got home, that's when Stormy finally shouted. And I had never been so devastated.

I had a hard time making sense of his words as quickly as they came; instead, I was focused on the fury of his red face and the volume of his criticism. But certain words and phrases were clear: "embarrassing" "tired of this shit" "the hell is wrong with you?"

At the end of his tirade, Stormy scowled and gave a good kick to the couch. Then he marched into his room and slammed his door shut. I remained standing there, lower lip twitching, shoulders heaving up and down. *It was a good story,* I thought. *The one about Stormy loving me.*[31]

---

[31] When I conducted an interview with Stormy on June 23rd of this year, Stormy made it very clear that he did not think that Lizzy was mentally ill, despite the incident at Nicole's house and despite the apparent hallucinations and/or delusions that followed the incident.

CHAPTER 8

It was the following night that I decided to run away. That day had been as awful as the previous one, maybe worse. Instead of shouting at me and making me feel small, now Stormy was ignoring me and making me feel invisible. A few times I tried speaking to him, asking him to help me with homework or toss the football around, but he wouldn't say a word in response. He just looked right past me and walked away.

My mother, for her part, spent most of the evening in her bedroom, mascara smeared on her cheeks, mourning the loss of her ring if not her husband.

But that evening, shortly before bedtime, as I was eating a Pop Tart at the kitchen table, Stormy broke his silence. For a few minutes, he had been standing at the sink, back to me, drinking a glass of water. Occasionally, he'd rock back and forth, breathing deeply. I could tell he was still mad. Finally, he turned and faced me. When he spoke, his voice was quiet and restrained. "I spoke with Nicole today," he said.

"Yeah?"

"Yeah. She asked me to meet down at Ice Palace Park. So that's what I did."

I took another bite of my Pop Tart. Stormy was acting strange. "So what did she say? Is she still mad at me? Does she still think that I'm a little freak?"

Stormy smiled, but it was a bitter smile. "What she said was that she really likes me. She said that I was smart and handsome."

"That's good. That must have made you feel happy."

"And then she said that she couldn't be with me anymore. That she was breaking up with me."

I opened my mouth but nothing came out. I tried again. "That stinks," was all I could muster.

Stormy dumped the remaining water into the sink, walked over to where I was sitting, and bent down, inches from my face. "Here's the thing," he said, his voice still quiet, but now trembling. "She broke up with me because of you. Because you are a little freak. And I'll never, ever forgive you."

And that was it. He left the kitchen. I stared at the last piece of Pop Tart on my plate, but I'd lost my appetite. My brother's morsel of happiness was gone, and I'd been the one who'd taken it.

Don't get me wrong. In a way, I was glad. Nicole was out of the picture, just like I wanted her to be. But there was an unintended consequence, a terrible one at that—my brother's disapproval. I needed him more than ever, and now I worried that I would never have him again. I sat at the table for a long time, thinking, thinking. And as I sat there, one thing became very clear. I couldn't stand to be in the house. At least not tonight. My mother's contempt I could stomach, but not Stormy's.

So I decided that I'd leave. I'd fill a backpack with clothes and food, and I'd leave. I wouldn't come back tonight. Wouldn't come back tomorrow night. I pictured the two of them standing on the front porch, shaking heads and peering down the asphalt. "Where'd she go?" Mom would say, her voice slurred from booze. "When's she coming back?"

"I'm afraid the answer is never," Stormy would say. "I must have hurt her really bad with the things I said. And now I've gotta live with it for the rest of my life. I should have never shouted at my little Squirt. I should have never blamed her for my misery."

"And," my mother would say, "I should have never accused her of stealing that ring."

I thought some more, gaining a little clarity, and now I did stick the last piece of Pop Tart in my mouth. The way I figured things, I would stay away for two or three days. That would give my mother and my brother time to reflect on how much I meant to them. And when I came back, things would be different. Upon seeing me reappear in the glow of the streetlights, my mother would fall to her knees and raise her arms in the air. "Praise Jesus," she'd say. Then the tears would fall down her cheeks. "Praise Jesus, she's back."

And Stormy. He'd grab me and swing me round and round, all the while laughing and crying and talking at the same time. "I thought you were gone for good," he'd say. "I thought you'd left me all alone. Don't ever do that again, Lizzy. I can't bear the thought of losing you for even a minute more. You're my girl, and don't you ever forget it."

"I won't, Stormy, I won't!"

I packed quickly, without much of a plan. Two hoodies, two T-shirts, two pairs of jeans, two pairs of socks, two pairs of underwear. I packed my sketch pad and my journal. I packed *Frankenstein* by Mary Shelley. Toothbrush. Toothpaste. A flashlight. I stuffed all of it into my school backpack. Then I rolled up my sleeping bag. They'd miss me, all right.

From the kitchen, I snagged a loaf of bread, a bag of lunch meat, the remains of the peanut butter, a couple of apples, and a box of granola bars. I filled up my water bottle. Not a feast, but enough to survive for a couple days.

Mom was now in the living room, watching television, dead to the world. The lonely laugh track echoed off the walls. My brother was in his room. I wanted to say good-bye but it would be no good.

I tiptoed through the living room without saying a word. My

mother didn't look up. Maybe she never even noticed me. With a deep breath, I pushed open the door and stepped outside. The wind was cold and the sky was black.[32]

Backpack slung around my shoulders, sleeping bag in one hand, food bag in the other, I began walking. I knew exactly where I was going. I walked down Harrison Avenue, past the Manhattan Bar where a couple of drunks stumbled through the doorway shoulder-to-shoulder, past the run-down Presbyterian church where prayers were being swept into corners, past the Tennessee Pass Café where my mother slaved day after day after day. A few people passed me on the sidewalk, but none of them paid me any mind. Even though I had been outside for a total of ten minutes or less, my little world now seemed distant and trivial, somehow. I thought of Nicole and smiled. It had been silly to feel so jealous. She was just a girl. She'd done nothing wrong. There was nothing to worry about now. I walked and walked and walked until I was out of Leadville proper, and now there were only tired motels and hole-in-the-wall restaurants and closed-down auto shops.

After another half mile, there were no more businesses, instead just sheet metal and rotted wood collapsed over spoil heaps, the remnants of mining days gone. Without the streetlights of town, the world was very dark, but I kept my flashlight in my bag. Occasionally, a car would pass by, kicking up dirt, but mostly things were quiet and still. Despite the darkness, I knew the area well. Stormy, Shannon, and I came this way every summer to go hiking and camping and swimming. But I'd never been here this late at night. I'd never been here by myself.[33]

I came to County Road 11½ and turned north, the half-moon twisting in and out of swirling black clouds. Right about now my mother would be knocking on Stormy's door, saying, "Where

---

[32] It wasn't until an hour later that Jessica and Stormy realized Lizzy was gone. Jessica called Tabitha's house, but she wasn't there. Stormy searched the surrounding neighborhood without any luck.

[33] This is the same path she and her siblings took to go to Opal Lake the day Shannon died.

do you think your sister went? I heard the door shut an hour ago. Now she's gone, all gone."

I walked for another thirty minutes, and even though I was sure I was heading in the right direction, I began feeling more and more anxious when the trailhead didn't appear. Another half mile and I saw an abandoned house[34] barely visible in the moonlight, and that made me feel better because I had hidden near that house, many years ago, when I was just a child, while Stormy pretended he couldn't find me. Someday Stormy would forgive me. But until then...

I finally reached the trailhead for the Colorado-Midland trail. I glanced at my wristwatch and pressed the light-up button. It was 11:13. I wasn't tired, though. I pulled out an apple from my food bag and chewed it quickly then tossed the core on the ground.

I walked hurriedly, and above me the branches resembled scary skeleton bones trembling in the moonlight. And as I continued down the darkened path I decided that I was no longer just a little girl. Not anymore. I was on my own; out in the wild; free. From somewhere I could hear the sound of the river crashing against the shore. I could hear leaves rustling. I could hear the night animals scurrying and shrieking. It was disconcerting. I kept walking.

It was shortly before midnight when I finally stopped. My legs ached and so did my belly. The sky was covered with black clouds and the moon had disappeared. I was tired and figured I should get some sleep. I went off the path a ways and found a clearing hidden behind a group of darkened pine trees. This is where I would camp for the night. I would be safe here, I told myself, even though I didn't fully believe it. I unrolled my sleeping bag and struggled my way inside, shivering from fear as much as the cold. The ground was hard and bumpy, and I cursed

---

[34] But the house wasn't actually abandoned. A man named Horst Fischer lived there. More on him later.

myself for not bringing a pillow.[35]

I pulled out my flashlight and my book. For a while I read Frankenstein, and it resonated: *The whole series of my life appeared to me as a dream; I sometimes doubted if indeed it were all true, for it never presented itself to my mind with the force of reality.*

After twenty minutes or so, I closed the book and placed it against my chest. I breathed deeply and shut my eyes. Another few minutes and I must have fallen asleep. But I hadn't slept long when I was startled awake by a sound.

My eyes flew open and I tried orienting myself. I took a deep breath. And there was the sound again. How best to describe it? A long monotone whistling, almost like the distant cry of a train. But I knew that I was too far buried in the woods to hear the Southern Railroad. Maybe it was a nocturnal animal, ready to feast. I'd heard of travelers being attacked by mountain lions, picked apart by crows. Oh, stop it. Relax. I sat up in my sleeping bag and blew on my hands, which were turning numb in the cold autumn night. For a few seconds, the whistling stopped. I noticed that I was holding my breath and so I let it out. But then, once again, the whistling resumed.[36]

I thought about getting to my feet and running, making my way back to the trailhead. But then I told myself that I was being silly and that Stormy would laugh at my cowardice. It was just a sound after all. An owl maybe. I was in the woods. There were sounds in the woods. I forced a smile. I wasn't going home. Not tonight. More than anything, I wanted Stormy to miss me. More than anything, I wanted him to wonder where I was.

I tried again to sleep, but I knew that it was hopeless. Still, I forced myself to keep my eyes shut and to breathe deeply and to

---

[35] Lizzy's sleeping bag, food, and her copy of *Frankenstein* were recovered in the woods.
[36] In his stories, Mike Greiner described the Lantern Man as whistling "a single note, unchanging."

think happy thoughts. Like the time Stormy took turns giving me and Shannon piggyback rides and raced through the house making crazy siren sounds. Or the time we went swimming and Stormy lost his swimming trunks and refused to come out of the water until Shannon went home and got him a pair of jeans. He made us pinky promise never to tell a soul.

But after another few minutes I ran out of happy thoughts. So I just sat there in the darkness.

And that's when I saw the lantern.[37]

---

[37] Yes, a lantern. The Lantern Man. Not to spread ghost stories, but I would be remiss if I didn't mention that in the previous three decades there had been at least two mysterious unsolved deaths near the Midland Trail. And now three.

Figure 8: In the background is the copy of Frankenstein that Lizzy had been reading. In the foreground are photographs of Lizzy's recovered sleeping bag, Hagerman Tunnel, the Colorado-Midland Trail.

CHAPTER 9

I didn't know it was a lantern at first. I thought maybe it was campfire burning or a flashlight shining. What I knew for certain was that somebody was in the forest. Somebody other than me. While the light didn't seem to be getting any closer, it seemed to be getting brighter. And still there was the whistling.

I was scaring myself with irrational thoughts. I pulled my body out of my sleeping bag and crouched in my hiding place, trying to get a glimpse at the stranger. But all I could see was the glow of the light. I'm not sure where the courage (or maybe stupidity) came from, but I rose to my feet and started toward the glow. I walked as quietly as I could, but occasionally I would step on a branch or some dead leaves, and the forest would whisper a warning.

I had gotten within ten feet of the light, and now I could see that it was, indeed, a lantern, like the ones that miners from a hundred fifty years back would carry. And I knew at that moment that it was the Lantern Man, the one my father had warned me about, the one I had dreamed about. He was very tall and very thin. I would say eight feet tall or more, although I have never been a good judge of such things. He wore all black, including some sort of a cape, and he had long and straight gray hair that hung below his shoulders. His face was pale, almost translucent. But the most terrifying thing were his eyes: they were just cavernous holes, the eyes of a dead man.[38]

I was so stunned by his appearance that I just stood there, half paralyzed. He turned toward me and took a long step and then another. Fear overpowering my momentary inertia, I dropped to my knees and then my stomach. I remained on the forest floor, holding my breath, tears leaking from the corner of my eyes.

I waited for what seemed like a long time. When I finally turned my head and looked up, he was gone. But I could see his lantern waving back and forth, strange shadows dancing in the woods.

I remained on the ground, trembling and having a hard time catching my breath. More than ever, I thought that I'd made an awful mistake by running away from home and hiding out in these haunted hills. But then I thought of Stormy again and what he would say. "C'mon, Squirt. It's an adventure! It's not every day that you see a giant ghost tromping through the woods. Follow after him. Locate his evil lair. And then write a story about it. You're such a good storyteller! Such a good liar!"

I rose to my feet and stood there for several moments. The wind was blowing cold. When we were younger, Stormy, Shannon, and I used to come out here all the time, searching for hidden caves and maybe a bear. But that was during the daytime. That was when the sun shone and the world wasn't warped by darkness. "C'mon, Squirt. It's an adventure!" I took a deep breath and began walking, slowly at first, but then picking up the pace. For a while, the glow of the lantern was far off in the distance, but soon enough I'd made up ground and now the strange figure wasn't more than thirty yards away. Once again, I could hear him whistling soft and low.

I remembered what my father had said so many years ago: *He searches for children who have strayed from the path to keep him eternal company in his cold, abandoned tunnel.*

I kept following him, weaving in and out of the pine trees

---

[38] While auditory hallucinations are more common, there are various well-documented causes (schizophrenia, delirium, migraines, sleep disturbances, drug effects etc.) of visual hallucinations as well.

and deadened aspens. I was afraid I was going to lose my way, and a few times I stopped and shook my head and thought, *What the hell are you doing, little girl?* but each time I continued, drifting farther up the mountain and farther from home.

Eventually I came to a trail that seemed to have once been an old railroad bed. Some of the railroad cuts had collapsed and the trestles had rotted away. The Lantern Man didn't turn around, but I wondered if he knew that I was right there behind him.

Now it seemed that his whistling was getting louder, so much so that I had to cover my ears as I walked. I followed him up the steep incline. The moon had poked through the dark clouds, and I could better see his figure—like a count walking through the fog-filled streets of London.

And then, just like that, he vanished. Having seen too many horror movies, I quickly spun around, half-expecting him to leap out from behind me. But, no. He was gone.

I hurried upward until I located the spot from which he'd vanished. And there I came to a strange sight of a long tunnel blasted through the rock. In front of the tunnel was an old rotted wood sign. Hands trembling, I pulled out my flashlight and turned it on. Wide-eyed, I read the sign:

HAGERMAN TUNNEL

This is the east portal of the Hagerman Tunnel, the highest railroad tunnel in the world at the time of its completion in 1887. The great tunnel is 11,530 feet above sea level. It is 2,161 feet long, 16 feet high, 18 feet wide and cost $200,000. It was replaced in 1890-91 by the Bush-Ivanhoe (later Carlton) Tunnel further down the road to Leadville. The Hagerman Tunnel was used briefly again in 1898-99 but was soon abandoned.
DANGER! DON'T ENTER!

This is where the Lantern Man had disappeared, into an old abandoned railroad tunnel. The same place that he'd frozen to death so many years ago. It's strange, but my fear had disappeared, too. Here I was, alone in the middle of the mountains chasing after some strange ghost. But I wasn't scared.

To get down to the tunnel entrance, I had to get on my stomach and slide down a steep dirt wall, hardened with ice. As I descended, I could feel a jagged rock tear into my skin, but I simply gritted my teeth and continued on.

At the bottom, I got on my haunches and moved sideways like a crab. The floor to the tunnel was covered with dirty snow, and the walls and ceiling were thick with ice. I rose to a hunchback position and cautiously entered the tunnel. The breath came out of my mouth in puffs of steam. I took a few steps forward. The snow was deeper than I thought, coming nearly to my knees. Once again, I could hear the low, monotonous whistling. I walked. The farther inside the tunnel I got, the darker it became. I imagined Stormy saying, "Too bad you listened to me, Squirt. It's one thing to be brave. It's quite another to be a moron. You're entering the moron phase." I placed my hands against the frozen walls and continued forward, now blind but reluctant to use my flashlight.

It seemed that I moved slowly forward for an hour, but it was probably only a handful of minutes. Eventually, I came around a bend, and I again saw the shivering of light and heard the low whistle. His back was to me, and his cape was floating in the tunnel breeze. He wasn't more than ten yards away now, and if he'd turned around he'd have seen me and likely attacked me. But at that moment I didn't care. In fact, instead of spinning around and running or hiding in the shadows, I took another step forward.

And that's when I saw them. Girls. Some of them very young. Some of them my age or older. They were piled on top of one another, but they weren't dead, as I could hear moans and see movement. The Lantern Man stood over them, waving his lantern like he was trying to bless them. But there would be no salvation for those girls, not today, not ever.

I might have screamed. I might have. Because now my courage

was gone. Now my curiosity was sapped. This time I did turn and run, but not before slipping on the snow and ice. I moaned as I struggled to my feet. And as I staggered through the darkness, I was sure the Lantern Man was behind me, was sure I heard his whistling, was sure I saw flashes of light dancing beneath my feet. I might have screamed some more.

When I reached the edge of the tunnel and peered behind me, however, there was nobody there. The ghost, the monster, had stayed behind with his collected souls. I continued down the mountain, using the flashlight to guide my way.[39]

An hour later I reached the trailhead. And an hour after that I reached my house. It was nearing three in the morning, but all the lights were on. When I stepped inside, my mother was standing in the living room, her hair disheveled, a cigarette burning between her fingers. She was probably drunk. My brother stood directly behind her, his eyes red and swollen. My mother stared at me for a long moment, her lips trembling as if she were trying to say something but couldn't muster the energy. With resignation, she slumped down on the couch and closed her eyes. She took a final drag of her cigarette and crushed it out in an ashtray. Stormy, meanwhile, took a few steps forward.

"Where you been?" he said, his voice all gravelly.

"Out," I said. "In the hills."

"You shouldn't have done that. Not without telling us first."

"You were mad at me."

"We were getting ready to call the police. We didn't know what had happened. You had us both scared."

My mother remained on the couch, silent, but I knew she was angry, too. It was two against one. I wished my father was here.

"I saw the Lantern Man," I said.

"Who?"

---

[39] After Chloe Peterson's death, Detective Kline and several officers scoured Hagerman Tunnel for clues. While much evidence related to her homicide was collected (a pair of panties, hair, blood splatters), there was no evidence of a pile of tortured girls.

"The Lantern Man. The one Dad used to tell us about. He makes a strange whistling sound, just like Dad said. He kills girls and eats their flesh, just like Dad said. And I'm afraid I might be next."[40]

Figure 9: "From the Ruins" by Lizzy Greiner.

Figure 10: "Hagerman's Tunnel" by Lizzy Greiner.

The following is an excerpt from The Encyclopedia of Monsters, Ghouls, and Ogres *(edited by John F. King, Beatrice Owens, and Benjamin Kelly). The book was found in Lizzy's room, checked out from the library shortly after her visit to Hagerman Tunnel.*

Perhaps the earliest attempt at defining "monsters" came in ancient Babylonia where abnormal fetuses were categorized into groups dependent on the type of abnormality (e.g. six fingers on a hand). Since these types of malformations could not yet be explained by scientists, ancient people, understandably, believed these deformities were a sign of fury leveled by their gods. Beyond Babylonia, monsters came to represent the unknown, usually living in faraway and foreboding places, waiting, as it were, to torture and kill the innocent who became lost in the forest or desert or mountain. Eventually these shadowy monsters were imagined in works of literature and art and even commodified (as in P.T. Barnum's 19th Century circuses).

From a psychological lens, Carl Jung theorized that these monsters served to inhabit our collective imagination. He held that certain types of archetypes (such as the bogeyman) are present in virtually every person in every culture across the world. Interestingly, he believed that we are born programed with these archetypes in our consciousness, an innate fear that helps defines us as human beings. Throughout history, these types of archetypes can be seen in various depictions of evil such as the Lord of Darkness, the Grim Reaper, or Gollum. But how do we know that these are, in fact, archetypes, and that we haven't just learned about these monsters from literature, art, or religion? Perhaps the most compelling evidence can be found by analyzing young children's dreams. Children do not have to learn about the "bogeyman" to dream about him. They do not need to be taught to fear the blackened forest; they will fear it by instinct. It also seems that these so-called "shadow" archetypes are remarkably similar from culture to culture. Fantasy novelist Ursula Le Guin describes this archetypal symbol in this way: "The shadow is on the other side of our psyche, the dark brother of the conscious mind. It is Cain, Caliban, Frankenstein's monster, Mr. Hyde. It is Frodo's enemy Gollum. It is the Doppelgänger. It is the were-wolf, the wolf, the bear, the tiger of a thousand folktales; it is the serpent, Lucifer. The shadow stands on the threshold between the conscious and the unconscious mind, and we meet it in our dreams, as sister, brother, friend, beast, monster, enemy, guide."

Psychologists such as Wednell Harmon have argued that these monsters are essentially projections of ourselves, providing a representation of the qualities that we have repressed and denied. Allowing this awareness makes it possible to recognize ourselves as vital human beings and not simply two-dimensional characters. The person who denies his own profound relationship with evil denies his own humanness. Instead of seeing the monster as the "other," we must, therefore, explore our shared humanity through all of its viciousness and grotesqueness. It is impossible to have the light without the darkness, God without the devil, salvation without damnation.

And what are some of these monsters? In early Gaelic and Slavic folk tales, mysterious lights, believed to be malevolent spirits of the dead, wandered through secluded areas looking to destroy the souls of people who had lost their way. Often times, these lights were given human names such as Jack, Will or Joan. In most cases, the lights signified coming tragedy; however, in some tales the lights were not dangerous and would, in fact, lead people to vast treasures and riches.

Samuel Taylor Coleridge's 1798 poem "The Rime of the Ancient Mariner" seems to describe some version of these lights:

About, about in reel and rout,
The death-fires danced at night;
The water, like a witch's oil,
Burnt green, and blue and white

While these tales of wandering lighted souls can be traced back several hundred years, the specific legend of Lantern Men first became documented in 19th Century England. Lantern Men (sometimes called Will-o'-the-Wisps) were seen in the marshes around Wickerbough, located in Oltenshire. They were believed to be evil spirits trying to trick their victims into following them into the reed beds.

In recent years, scientists have developed a number of theories to try to explain the reports of these so-called Lantern Men. It has been theorized that the lights may have come from marsh gasses, which sometimes catch fire, making flames over boggy ground. Others have conjectured that the lights were actually ball lightning, an unexplained atmospheric phenomenon associated with thunderstorms that usually lasts much longer than a singular lightning bolt. In the past, of course, these scientific theories weren't yet developed, so people were rightfully frightened by the sight of mysterious lights moving from place to place on a dark night. It is entirely possible that some people, inquisitive, walked toward these lights and, unable to see, unwittingly fell into marshes or lakes, eventually drowning.

However, while these theories might explain the vision of the night glow, they do nothing to explain the numerous sightings of the Lantern Man himself. Perhaps these stories are imagined or fabricated, but it is interesting to note how many similar reports there have been in disparate locations across the globe. While initially most of these sightings were in Europe, in the 20th Century and into the 21st Century, there have been a multitude of eyewitness reports in the United States as well. Here are a few examples: in 1922, a fisherman from Portland, Maine, claimed to have seen a strange man carrying a lantern near a wharf. As the stranger moved closer, his lantern glowing in the night, the fisherman could hear the sound of whistling. Fearful, he ran down the pier and hid in a fishing boat. After several minutes, he finally peered out of the boat and the man had vanished. However, when he looked behind him, he saw that the lantern was now in the boat with him. He panicked and knocked the lantern over, starting a fire in the boat. The fisherman survived but claimed that the Lantern Man had tried killing him by fire.

More than thirty years later, in Stillwood, Michigan, a young girl claimed that a tall and slender man carrying a lantern and whistling a single note followed her for nearly a mile while she walked her dog along the riverbank. Her dog, sensing danger, pulled away from the girl and ran toward the figure, but he disappeared into the mist. Unfortunately, the dog vanished, too, and the girl could not locate him. The following morning, her father found the dog, not far from where she'd been walking, lying on the riverbank, having drowned in the water.

In 1978, a woman from Holcomb, Kansas, had gone to the store to get food for dinner. After shopping, she hurried down the empty streets, past the run-down brick buildings of downtown, clutching a bag full of groceries, looking this way and that. Lights shone from streetlamps and behind windows, and she quickened her pace, but then, from behind her, she heard footsteps on the pavement getting louder and louder. She spun around and saw that it was a man who carried an old-fashioned mining lantern that swung back and forth with each step he took. She tried escaping, but he was on her. He grabbed her arm and the bag fell to the ground. A red apple rolled down the sidewalk and then another one. He held the lantern to his face and she saw that his skin was burnt by fire and his eyes were empty holes. He pinned her to the ground and his lantern shattered next to her head. But this woman was fiercer than you might think, and she was able to gather her strength and reach for his lantern. She swung it toward his skeletal arms and the lantern shattered, the flame catching on his decaying skin. The monster screamed in pain and released the poor woman from his grasp. And so it is commonly believed that Lantern Men can be wounded, perhaps killed, by fire.

In more recent times, the so-called Lantern Man has been reported to be seen in the Colorado mountains near the old mining town of Leadville. In that myth, it is believed that he was originally a miner during the 1880s and died while constructing the now-abandoned railroad tunnel known as the Hagerman Tunnel.

If you even run into this evil spirit, perhaps you should heed the following advice that was written in a pamphlet by an Englishman named Lucas Bromwell back in 1891. Maybe the advice will save your life!

1. Never carry your own lantern or torch. Lantern Men are attracted to light.
2. Never whistle. He will run toward the whistle and suffocate you.
3. If caught in his light, hold your breath. Otherwise he can take it away for good.
4. Never, ever mock a Lantern Man. He will always seek revenge.
5. The only way to kill a Lantern Man is by setting him on fire.[41]

---

[41] According to Stormy, Lizzy began keeping makeshift torches and fuel close to her bed when she slept. Her mother knew nothing of this.

The following are transcribed newspaper articles that have the following elements in common: 1) Hagerman Tunnel, 2) a man carrying a lantern, and 3) a missing girl.

LEADVILLE DAILY HERALD
LEADVILLE, CO. WEDNESDAY, APRIL 21, 1887

DISAPPEARED

A Young Woman Suddenly Disappears and No
Clues to Her Whereabouts
Are Found

On last Thursday evening, Mrs. Edith Wasson arrived in this city from Buena Vista, accompanied by her husband, Mr. Ryan Wasson, a gentleman of thirty-three years of age, who was paying his first visit to Leadville. Both the gentleman and his wife stayed at the Windsor Hotel but spent a large portion of their time near the new Hagerman Tunnel, where Mr. Wasson has been hired as an engineer.

On last Saturday, it had been decided that the gentleman should travel by horse from the east slope of Hagerman Pass to the west side from which the tunnel might be faster to construct. Mr. Wasson encouraged his wife to join him for the travel but feeling unwell she remained on the east side in the Colorado-Midland Railroad campsite.

Early that evening, Mrs. Wasson informed several of the tunnel engineers that she was going to take a stroll along the creek. Since that time the woman has failed to appear back at the campsite, and despite the fact that a search party was instantly instituted, and that numerous and diligent inquiries have been made, no clue to her whereabouts have been established. Detectives have been employed and the police notified of the disappearance, but with no favorable results, and Mr. Ryan Wasson even visited the various hospitals and undertaking establishments in person, in search for his lost wife.

Several theories are given for the cause of the woman's disappearance—among them that she was taken ill in the woods and was unable to return to the campsite, while another is that she was taken by force, as an unknown man has been reported wandering in the area. Descriptions of the man varied, but most agreed that he was tall and thin and carried a lantern, likely the type to be used in one of the many mines in the area. The former theory is generally accepted as the true one, however, and the fact of the indisposition of the woman on the day of her disappearance tends to give it credence.

Additional detectives were employed yesterday, and it is expected that the missing woman will be brought to light in a few days.[42]

---

[42] I could find no other records of Mrs. Edith Wasson.

DAILY LEADVILLE TIMES
LEADVILLE, COLORADO; TUESDAY, AUGUST 15, 1973

HONOR ROLL STUDENT GOES MISSING
by Ernie Walford

LEADVILLE, August 15—A local girl has gone missing in the woods outside of Leadville.

16-year-old Annie Gaddis has been missing since Monday evening when the friends she went camping with left her alone while they searched for firewood. When they returned, Annie had vanished. After searching for nearly two hours, the girls returned to town and informed the local authorities of her disappearance.

Annie is described as white, tall and thin, with blue eyes and long, dark hair. When she was last seen, she was wearing black sweatpants and a denim jacket.

While several search parties have been organized to search for the missing girl, so far they have not found any signs of her.

Annie suffers from depression and is prone to drink alcohol. Her friends say that she had been drinking heavily that night, which is the reason she didn't join them when they left their campsite, near Hagerman Tunnel, to search for wood. Her friend Grace Patterson told reporters that she had talked about hurting herself earlier that night. "I wish we had taken her more seriously. I'm afraid she might have done something."

However, her mother, Maureen Gaddis, doesn't believe that's the case. "Annie was in a very good place. She had climbed her way out of the deep hole she'd been in and had been making great progress in school and in her relationships. I don't believe she would have harmed herself."

The Leadville Police Department has opened up a hotline where people can call in any tips, no matter how seemingly insignificant.

"The longer this drags on, the less likely we are to find her unharmed," Chief Officer Bill Hicks said. "The woods are a very dangerous place for anybody to be on their own, much less for a young girl. We're asking anybody who has any information whatsoever on her whereabouts to report it to our hotline or directly to our department. We will continue to search for her as long and as hard as humanly possible."

The police are also asking for any information on a man seen by the girls near the campsite. He is described as being tall and thin with shoulder-length blonde hair. He was carrying what is believed to be an old-fashioned mining lantern. The man is not a suspect, but rather a person of interest.[43]

---

[43] The body of Annie Gaddis was never found, and the case remains unsolved. I had hoped to interview her parents but learned that they are both deceased: Maureen Gaddis passed in 1991, and her husband, Tom Gaddis, in 2002. I did secure contact information for a Grace Patterson Miller of Sterling, Colorado, whom I believe to be the friend mentioned in the article. For several weeks, Mrs. Miller did not return my phone calls. Then on July 26th of this year, she did call me back. See note 89 for details on our conversation.

LEADVILLE TODAY
LEADVILLE, COLORADO; SATURDAY, JULY 6, 1986

FRANTIC SEARCH FOR MISSING GIRL
by Charles T. Howard

LEADVILLE, July 6—A frantic search is underway for a missing 12-year-old girl who disappeared over the weekend after getting separated from her family hiking the Colorado-Midland Trail, near the abandoned Hagerman Tunnel.

Donna Roswell was last seen by her parents at about 12:30pm on Saturday. She went off the trail to search for a walking stick. When she didn't return after several minutes, her parents called her name and went searching for her but couldn't locate her.

Yesterday, nearly fifty volunteers joined police officers and members of the forest department to search through the night for any trace of the missing girl.

Donna is described as white, about 4 ft 11 ins tall, around 95 pounds with blue eyes and blond hair, which she was wearing in a ponytail. She was wearing blue jeans, a distinctive pink sweatshirt with the Colorado state flag insignia on the front, brown hiking boots, and a silver and black backpack.

Her father, Dan Roswell, said, "It just isn't like her to go wandering off by herself. Even though she's only 12, she's very

responsible and I don't see how she could have become disoriented. We're trying to stay positive. We love her so much and
just want her to come home safely."

In addition to the search parties, nearly a hundred people
met at the Community Church of Leadville to help organize more
search parties and distribute fliers. Bloodhounds are also being
gathered to try and pick up Donna's scent.

While there are no suspects in the case, authorities are on the
lookout for a man who had been seen the previous night by
other campers. The man startled a man and a woman by shining a mining lantern in their faces, shouting, and then disappearing into the woods. He is described as being of medium
height and build. He was wearing a blue or black stocking cap
and a camouflage shirt.

Brooke Halpern, whose daughter is a friend of Donna's, told
CBS news: "Everybody who knows Donna loves her. We're
going to search everywhere we can possibly think of. To think
that somebody might have hurt her—it's too terrible to think
of."[44]

---

[44] Like Annie Gaddis, Donna was never heard from again, and her body was
never found. Her mother committed suicide two years later. Her father, Dan
Roswell, still lives in Leadville, on W. 8th Street, not far from Evergreen
Cemetery. It is the same house that Donna grew up in. Mr. Roswell is now in
his early sixties and recently retired from his job at the Climax Mine. He
agreed to sit down with me for an interview. Due to physical issues, he was
unable to come to the police station, so, instead, I went to his house. Our
interview took place on July 5th, twenty-two years to the day Donna went
missing. Following is a portion of the transcript of our conversation.

PERSON INTERVIEWED: DAN ROSWELL
DATE OF INTERVIEW: JULY 5, 2008
TIME OF INTERVIEW: 11:15 A.M.
CASE NUMBER: 06-002050
INTERVIEW CONDUCTED BY: DET. RUSS BUCHANAN
TRANSCRIBED BY: MELISSA HOWELL

BUCHANAN: And what do you remember about that day?

ROSWELL: Everything. I remember every goddamn thing.

BUCHANAN: Twenty-two years ago.

ROSWELL: That's right. Twenty-two years ago. Might as well be twenty-two hours ago.

BUCHANAN: Your family went hiking.

ROSWELL: It was Fourth of July weekend. Donna loved hiking. Most kids don't. She always loved it. She just loved being outside with nature.

BUCHANAN: And you took the Midland Trail.

ROSWELL: That's right. We'd hiked on that trail many times before. On that day, there was hardly anybody else on the trail. The sky was blank blue and the sun was shining. Donna was laughing and skipping like she was bound to do. She wore a T-shirt with the Colorado state flag insignia on the front.

BUCHANAN: The newspaper report said it was a sweatshirt.

ROSWELL: No, mister. It was a T-shirt. I remember because I bought it for her. She wore that T-shirt a lot.

BUCHANAN: And how long had you been hiking before she got lost?

ROSWELL: Not long at all. Just a few minutes. She needed to use the bathroom. She stepped off the trail. I must have been a bit distracted. I was talking to Mary about something. I don't remember what. Maybe three minutes went by and then Mary asked what was taking Donna so long. I followed after her to make sure she was okay. I didn't see her anywhere. I called her name. I wasn't scared. Not right away. I thought she was hiding maybe. But then I called her name again and again. She didn't answer. One minute she's right there and then...

BUCHANAN: But you didn't hear anything? Screams? Sounds of struggling?

ROSWELL: No.

BUCHANAN: And then you and your wife started searching for her. You must have been panicked.

ROSWELL: You try not to think about the worst. But I was.

BUCHANAN: How long did you and your wife search for her until you went and got help?

ROSWELL: I don't know. Two hours, maybe? I stayed out there while Mary went and looked for help. Eventually the Forest Service. And then the next day volunteers. But it was no use. There was little to no organization, and the mountains were too vast. They never found her. Just found one of her shoes.

BUCHANAN: The newspaper article mentions a man with a lantern who had been scaring campers in the previous nights. But the police report is incomplete. Do you know anything about him?

ROSWELL: Yes, sir. I believe he's the one who killed my daughter.

BUCHANAN: Really?

ROSWELL: To some people, stories of the Lantern Man are just for fun. You know, ghost stories meant to scare your kids. But for me, he's more than a ghost. More than a boogeyman. He's the one who stole my daughter. He's the one who killed her.

BUCHANAN: How can you be so sure?

ROSWELL: The newspaper didn't report everything.

BUCHANAN: No?

ROSWELL: The people who saw him the night before told the police some other things. Some things that the Lantern Man was shouting.

BUCHANAN: What was he shouting?

ROSWELL: Well. He was threatening to kill them. And...he was threatening to eat them.

BUCHANAN: Okay. But I don't understand what—

ROSWELL: Here's why that's significant. A couple months later, I got an anonymous letter.

BUCHANAN: And you think it was from him?

ROSWELL: I know it was from him.

BUCHANAN: Why?

ROSWELL: Because in the letter he said that he'd stolen my girl. And he said that he'd eaten her.

dear mr roswell mabe you hav herd abot
albert fish and how he went to china and
there was a famin and how he lerned to eat
humin flesh and then wen he came back
he livd at 409 e 100 stret and he went to
406 w 15 stret and brot the mom pot chese
and strawberes and they had lunch and
then grace sat on his lap and kissd him so
he decid to eat her and thats wat he did
but furst he told her mom that he was taking her to a partee and he got a howse in
wistchistr and wile she piked flowrs he got
neked becus he didnt want to get blud on
them then he calld her and she crid becus
he was neked but he strippd her and chokd
her and cut her and cookd her so she was
tendr and ate her and i stole yur gurl and
what was her name donna and for five days
i rapd her and she scremed but her screms
got softr and softr and i decid id eat her just
like fish so i did but he was rong she didnt
taste good more like underooked chiken but
mabe i didnt coke her long enugh im not
sory for wut i done cuz i enjoid mysef sum
yor frend

Figure 11: The letter and photograph that Dan Roswell claims the
Lantern Man sent him. Albert Fish was an American serial killer who
lived from 1870-1936. He was a suspect in at least five murders, but
he claimed to have raped and eaten at least a hundred children.

PART 2

CHAPTER 10

Stormy wasn't surprised that I'd seen the Lantern Man. It was my imagination, he said. Or maybe my psychosis.

He reminded me of my past. As if youthful terrors could prove mental illness. When I was a little girl, he said, I used to swear that a strange woman had sneaked into Shannon's and my bedroom and was hiding behind the walls. I described her so vividly: black hair that fell below her waist; pale blue eyes; and most strangely, a nightmarish scarecrow resting on her shoulder. Stormy would have to walk around our room, tapping on the walls, warning the strange woman to stay away, that he would slice her throat if she appeared during the night. That seemed to comfort me and eventually I stopped talking about her.

There were others that came later, though. Like the preacher in the bowler's hat who followed me through the quiet streets, disappearing into an alleyway every time I spun around. Or the bloody baby, trapped in the attic, sobbing into the vents.[45]

So, no, he wasn't surprised that I'd seen the Lantern Man (especially after all of Dad's stories from so many years ago). But what did surprise him, I guess, was the intensity of the obsession. At school, I no longer tried completing my assignments. Instead, I would draw pictures of the Lantern Man. Or write stories about him. At home, it was even worse. I barely came

---

[45] Stormy downplayed these childhood "hallucinations." Jessica Greiner claimed she knew nothing about them.

out of my room at all. If Stormy pressed his ear to the door, he would have only heard the scraping of pencil against paper. Minute after minute. Hour after hour.[46]

The stories, the drawings, made Mom angry. She couldn't tell if I was creative or crazy. "Enough with the Lantern Man!" she shouted one day. "He's not real. Don't you know that, Lizzy?"

And Stormy would do his best to reassure her. "It's just a phase she's going through," I overheard him say once. "It's her way of coping with all her personal demons."

"A thousand drawings at least. And all those stories. It's not normal."

No, it wasn't normal. So they sent me to that doctor.[47]

Her name was Dr. Yuren, and it was supposed to be pronounced your-en, with the emphasis on the first syllable, but I have an immature sense of humor, so I pronounced it Dr. Urine.[48] And the funny thing is, I swear to God that's the way she smelled. Maybe it was just because she was old (60? 70?) or maybe it was because she had a bladder problem. In any case, spending time with her made me that much surer that I didn't want to grow old. I couldn't see a single advantage to it. Sure, you get to tell all the young kids about the good old days and stuff like that. But is that worth suffering from chronic pain, having hair grow in strange places, and smelling like Dr. Urine? I don't think so.

Her office was on Front Street in a little one-story brick building. She shared the space with a dentist named Dr. Francis.

---

[46] A small number of the drawings are included in this report. Lizzy actually left behind hundreds of them, but including all of them would have been redundant.

[47] The school referred Lizzy to go see Dr. Waugh. Jessica Greiner was reluctant because of the high cost and because she was cynical that a head shrink could cure her daughter. As Lizzy's behavior became more and more strange, however, she relented.

[48] Her name was Dr. Waugh, not Dr. Yuren.

I saw him once when I was leaving and he smiled at me and his teeth were yellow which didn't give me much confidence in him as a professional. Dr. Yuren's teeth, meanwhile, were white but crooked. She had long gray hair and always wore a long flower dress and long dangly earrings that I wanted to tear from her ears. The first time I met her, she smiled broadly like we were best buds and stuck her hand out to shake mine. I gave her one of my famous "dead fish" handshakes and then followed her into her office, the walls of which were covered with photographs of flowers. Seriously, there must have been two dozen of them. She must have really fucking liked flowers, I guess. I didn't tell her that I'd always hated flowers because it was an irrational hatred and would have made her question my sanity right then and there. I wanted to wait a few minutes before she questioned my sanity.

The other feature in her office was a feng shui water fountain, which was supposed to soothe but instead just made me need to pee all the time. Come to think of it, maybe Dr. Yuren had the same problem and that's why she smelled like her name.

There were three chairs, and she told me I could sit in any one I chose. I figured it was a psychological test of some sort. Sit on the leather recliner and it would show that you've got daddy issues. Sit on the soft blue chair and you burn ants with a magnifying glass. Sit on the red one and you're well adjusted. Well. I chose the ant-burning chair.

She sat down on the red chair (well-adjusted), crossed her legs, licked her fingers, and turned the page in her legal pad. I sat there staring straight ahead, chewing nervously on my lower lip.

She smiled that crooked smile and said, "Lizzy, it's wonderful to have you here. I've heard a lot about you. Do you want something to drink? Water? Apple juice?"

I shook my head, no. I could have used some of Mom's Southern Comfort, but I didn't say that.

Then, more pleasantries: "I like the dress you're wearing. It's very bright."

Yes, I was wearing a dress. And, yes, it was very bright (sort of a canary yellow). But I certainly didn't appreciate her talking to me like I was a special-needs child. "Yes," I said. "It's yellow." And that was all I said about that.

She studied her new subject for a few long moments and then said, "Lizzy, do you understand why you're here?"

I shrugged my shoulders. "Because my mom couldn't afford anybody good?"

She laughed, but it didn't sound genuine. "I can already tell that you're a clever girl, Lizzy."

"I'm not really clever," I said. "But I know why I'm here."

"And why do you think?"

"Because my mother thinks I'm crazy. And so do my teachers."

And now the doctor put on her nice act. She smiled like they smile. She spoke in a soft voice like they do. "Oh, no, Lizzy. They don't think you're crazy."

"No? Then what about you? Do you think I'm crazy?"

"No. Not even a little bit."

"I don't believe you. This office is sterile. It's meant for crazy people."

"Oh, come on," she said. "It's not so bad. The reason you're here, Lizzy, is because people are very concerned about you. Your mother especially. And the teachers at school."

I laughed out loud because it was funny, so damn funny.

"Why are you laughing?" she asked.

"Because you said that my mother is concerned about me."

"Oh, but she is. Very."

"And because you said the teachers at school are concerned about me."

"You don't think they are?"

Now I knew that this doctor was phony. That she hadn't done any research.

"Up until a few weeks ago," I said, "they didn't even know my name."

"But now they do?"

As if that proved her point. "Yeah. Now they do."

"And why, if I may ask, do you think that's the case?"

I glared at her. I wanted a cigarette. Wanted some booze. Wanted a double dose of dope shot into the webbings of my feet. "Because I beat up a girl, that's why."

She jotted some things down in her notebook. Or maybe she was just pretending to write. Then she glanced up and said, "That'll make you famous, all right."

"It was fun," I said. "Lots."

Time to pry. To find out what made me tick.

"Tell me about it," Dr. Pee Pee said. "Why was it fun?"

"Because she's the type of girl who make your eyes bleed."

"That's quite a description."

And now I wanted to talk about it. Wanted to talk about how much rage I had building inside of me. Because of my sister dying. Because of my father leaving me.[49]

"Her name is Sierra," I said. "She wears a shit-load of makeup and lipstick and has enormous cans. But that's not why I hit her. I hit her because she kept talking about me and laughing at me."

"And why was she laughing at you?"

I took a deep breath. I could feel my heart trying to escape my rib cage. "I don't know. Maybe I'm a clown. That must be it. I'm a clown."

She jotted down some more notes. And then she decided to go all moralistic because that's what adults do. She said, "I can understand you getting angry at Sierra because she was laughing at you. But do you think hitting her was the best choice?"

---

[49] "Lizzy suffers from abandonment issues," Dr. Waugh wrote. "The trauma of losing her sister and her father might lead to long-term psychological challenges due to a fear that abandonment will recur. The mood swings and anger are not surprising. Likely she suffers from anxiety and codependence (primarily exhibited with her brother). My diagnosis is Borderline Personality Disorder. DBT (Dialectical behavior therapy) may be necessary." Waugh also mentioned that medication would be advisable, but she never did prescribe it.

As if I were a second grader. I looked her in the eyes and said, "Yes. It was the best choice."

"Why?"

Her goddamn feng shui fountain was making me need to use the bathroom. Pissing my pants was a real possibility. "Sometimes," I said, "it's the only way you can get them to listen."

She kept on sermonizing. "But did you try talking things out first?"

"What the hell is this? Kindergarten?"

"Talking isn't just for kindergarteners. Isn't that what we're doing?"

"Only because they're making me. And I need to use the bathroom."

Dr. Yuren watched me for a moment, maybe taking a quick glance at my crotch to make sure I really did need to pee. "Okay," she said. "Right down the hall."

I rose from my seat and walked out of the room and into the hall. As I stepped into the bathroom, I realized that I was having trouble breathing, that maybe I was having an anxiety attack. Wasn't this bitch supposed to be soothing my anxiety? I sat down on the toilet and the pee gushed out and that made me a feel a bit better. I wiped myself and then pulled up my underwear. I splashed water on my face because that's what panicking people did in the movies. And as I stared at that face, I realized just how ugly it was. No wonder I'd never had a boyfriend. No wonder my brother was pushing away. I was hideous. And the things I'd done. The things I was still to do.

Back in the office and Dr. Yuren hadn't moved an inch. Her legs were crossed the same way and everything. Actually, it was kind of creepy. I sat down again and I wished I was somewhere else.

She talked some more. "I know you're close to your brother."

"Sometimes."

"So why did you run away? You know, he was terrified. And so was your mother."

It was a fair question, but I didn't want to answer. "Because."

"Did you want to terrify them?"

"Yes."[50]

The doctor kept pressing. I felt sorry for whomever was married to her. Not just because she smelled like piss but because she never stopped talking. I don't like people who never stop talking. They've got something to hide.

"I'm told this had something to do with your brother's girl-friend. Is that right?"

"Yes," I said. "But she's gone now."

She raised her eyebrows. "What do you mean?"

"She left him. Because of me. Because I slept in her bed. Just like Goldilocks."

"And are you glad?"

"Glad about what?"

"Glad that she left him?"

"I want my brother to be happy," I said, and that was the truth.

"And is he happy?"

I was getting tired of her. I was going to call her husband and ask him how the fuck he stayed with her. "I don't want to talk about it, anymore."

She looked at me with those pale blue eyes and said, "Fine. Let's talk about something else. Let's talk about the Lantern Man."

I knew it was coming, but I was still caught off guard. "Oh, boy," I said. "Here we go."

"What do you mean?"

"You're just like everybody else. You think I'm a liar."

She played dumb. "No, I don't. I never said that."

I wanted to punch her. I wanted to rip off those earrings. I wanted to take a bite of her olden flesh.

"Then why the hell are you asking me about the Lantern Man?"

---

[50] Dr. Waugh wrote, "Lizzy is also exhibiting attention-seeking behavior (e.g. the fight, running away). Often times she feels invisible and powerless. After all, she was unable to save her sister. She was unable to prevent her father from leaving. She wants to prove that she exists and can have an impact on other people (even if it's a negative impact)."

"Well...it's quite a story. I've heard about your description of him. And I've seen your artwork. He seems frightening."

She was patronizing me. I hated her as much as I hated flowers. "He is frightening," I said.

"But is he real, Lizzy? Is the Lantern Man real?"[51]

That was the question, wasn't it? There's lots of black magic in the world. Why not the Lantern Man?

"You mean, am I crazy? That's what you really mean, isn't it?"

My time was up, but Dr. Yuren kept talking. A real break-through, she assumed, was just moments away. "No, no. I never said that. I just want to know what's going on in your brain."

My brain is a traveling carnival, scaring all the children and old folk alike.

"Is he real?" I asked. "Are thoughts real? If thoughts are real then the Lantern Man is real."

He drags them into his tunnel. He sucks the soul from their mouth. He leaves their bodies for the maggots and murders of crows.

"Okay, fine," she said. "So you've seen him in your mind. But not in the real world."

"My brain is the real world. That's the big problem."

"I don't think I understand."

But I was on a roll. "Have I seen him in the woods? Did I follow him into Hagerman's Tunnel? Who's to say?"

"Who's to say?" asked the doctor. "What do you mean by that?"

"Who's to say anything about anything?"

Dr. Pee-Pee was getting frustrated. But my time was up. I didn't want to pay extra. "Right now you're acting very clever. But what I need from you is—"

---

[51] Dr. Waugh wrote: "I remain unsure about the genesis of this obsession. Perhaps it is simply more of the attention-seeking behavior I mentioned earlier. Of that, I am actually hopeful. Because if these visions and beliefs stem from powerful and irresistible hallucinations, then we will have a much deeper problem on our hands."

"You don't need a thing from me," and now I was shouting. "You don't know me. Not until forty-five minutes ago had you ever even seen me. So don't try to get into my head. I'm the only one allowed up there."

She slapped at her notebook. "I'm only trying to help, Lizzy. But for me to help, I need you on board. Does that make sense? We're on the same team."

"You're not on my team." Piss pants.

"I am. I promise you. I am."

"The Lantern Man is real." It just slipped out of my mouth. I didn't regret it.

"Now you're confusing me."

"He's real," I said. "Outside of my brain. He's real."

I knew she wouldn't believe me. Crazy, crazy, crazy.

"Okay. Then you saw him? In the mountains?"

"I'm done talking about the Lantern Man."

"Are you sure? Is there anything else you want to talk about?"

"No," I said. "I don't want to talk. Ever again."

She sat there for a long time, just staring at me. She was confused and sad. Because if I refused to talk, she couldn't fuck me up anymore, and that's what she was paid the big bucks to do.

Finally, she spoke. "Okay. No more talking then. But I know you're a phenomenal writer. How about writing your story instead?" I didn't bite. I kept my lips sealed. "I think you can do that, Lizzy. You have an insight unusual for your age. What do you think? Write it all down. And even if you take liberties with some details, you can keep the *essence* of the truth."

And now I spoke, and my lips were curled into a snarl. "Truth?" I said. "Who the fuck has time for that?"[52]

---

[52] I was skeptical that the Lantern Man represented any type of truth. But I pursued some leads. I learned that the detective in charge of the Donna Roswell case was a man named Alan Lindberg. Mr. Lindberg is in his early seventies and retired from the force. He lives in St. Petersburg, FL, but I spoke with him over the phone. See the following pages for a portion of our interview.

Figure 12: From Dr. Waugh's notebook. Shared with permission.

PERSON INTERVIEWED: ALAN LINDBERG
DATE OF INTERVIEW: JULY 7, 2008
TIME OF INTERVIEW: 02:55 P.M.
CASE NUMBER: 06-002050
INTERVIEW CONDUCTED BY: DET. RUSS BUCHANAN (PHONE)
TRANSCRIBED BY: MELISSA HOWELL

BUCHANAN: What do you remember about the case?

LINDBERG: I remember the girl well. Donna Roswell. Pretty little thing. Used to throw a baton in the Fourth of July parade. Truth be told, my own son had a little crush on her. When she went missing, it seemed like the whole town shut down. It was all anybody could talk about.

BUCHANAN: But the body was never found? No real breaks?

LINDBERG: No. Nothing. Hell, the whole case was a strange one. That a girl could just disappear like that. Right under her parents' eyes. Heartbreaking.

BUCHANAN: Do you think she was abducted?

LINDBERG: Could have been. Don't know for certain. Like I said. It was a strange case.

BUCHANAN: What about her parents? Were they suspects?

LINDBERG: The parents are always our first suspects. You know that, Russ.

BUCHANAN: But?

LINDBERG: But nothing. They could have done it. I don't know.

BUCHANAN: I spoke with Mr. Roswell recently.

LINDBERG: Is that so?

BUCHANAN: He also talked about a mystery man. A fellow that was spotted in the woods the night before. A man with a lantern.

LINDBERG: Sure. The Lantern Man. Leadville's own boogeyman. Every town's got one, right?

BUCHANAN: Anything to the story? Did you ever find him? There was mention of him in the local paper at the time.

LINDBERG: Never did. But then ghost hunting wasn't a part of my job description.

BUCHANAN: So you don't believe he had anything to do with the disappearance?

LINDBERG: Hell, Russ. It was a long time ago. Things get mixed up in my mind.

BUCHANAN: I don't believe that for a second, Detective.

LINDBERG: Believe what you want to believe. But to answer your question. We never found the Lantern Man. All we got were a few stories. Legends. None of them verified. Of course, the father said he received a letter.

BUCHANAN: Yes. He showed me a copy.

LINDBERG: If you ask me, somebody was pulling a mean-spirited prank on the Roswells. That's what I think. Or, perhaps Mr. Roswell himself wrote it.

BUCHANAN: Why would he do that?

LINDBERG: Because we all need a narrative. Something to get us through the day.

CHAPTER 11

Before I'd run away, before I'd become fixated on the Lantern Man, Stormy had been absolutely furious with me, and I suppose I can't blame him. After all, I'd done my best to sabotage his first real relationship with that Goldilocks stunt. But once I returned from my evening in the mountains, the anger seemed to dissipate. I was his little squirt, he told me. I'd always be his little squirt. And once he saw the pictures that I'd drawn and once he heard the stories that I'd told, he became downright concerned. He didn't want me to hurt. He didn't want me to be consumed by anxiety. Of course, he didn't believe that I had actually seen the Lantern Man. "He's not real, Squirt. You know that, right?" Instead, he thought it was my way of coping. Creating a real-life demon to replace my inner ones. That night he smoothed back my hair and said, "Listen, Lizzy. I know things have been tough on you. They've been tough on all of us. But just know that I'll always be here for you. Always."[53]

But with Nicole, the anger remained. What excuse, he asked me, did she have for rejecting him? What trauma had she experienced? She lacked empathy, he decided. She couldn't under-

---

[53] While Lizzy presents her relationship with her brother as a very intimate one ("I'd always be his little squirt"), in reality, by all accounts, Stormy had felt much closer to his other sister, Shannon. He also frequently expressed irritation and anger with Lizzy behind her back. He told Nicole that Lizzy was "immature" and that she "never leaves me alone." Additionally, he said that he "wished she'd get a boyfriend so she'd stop stalking me."

stand that I was different, that I hadn't meant any harm by sneaking into her house and sleeping beneath her covers. And then he said something that made me cringe. "She told me that she doesn't feel safe around you. She worries what you'll do next time."

In math class, he sat directly behind her, and on more than one occasion he imagined placing his hands around her slender neck and squeezing, squeezing, until she was coughing and gagging and dying. And I figured if he wouldn't do it, then maybe I could help him out.

Stormy told me he knew that he needed to shake away those thoughts. Because he wasn't a violent person, not really. Unlike me, he'd never even been in a fight. And, of course, he would never hurt a girl, especially someone like Nicole.[54]

But high schoolers talk, high schoolers gossip. And so they gossiped about Stormy and Nicole. "Poor Stormy," they whispered. "I heard he caught her sleeping with some frat boy," they said to each other, all behind cupped hands and with furtive expressions. And when he'd look their way, they'd quickly become mutes, pretend to be organizing papers or kicking open lockers.

And then there was this one boy. Josh Lange. A big boy. Football player. Flat top. Red face. Stormy and he used to be good friends. They played basketball and football together. But they weren't really friends anymore. Which is why Stormy was surprised when Josh approached him in the cafeteria that day.[55]

You see, he had a proposition for Stormy. A proposition that had to do with Chloe Peterson, that hot little thing who was in

---

[54] There is no evidence that Stormy felt these angry and homicidal thoughts about Nicole. However, he did write his share of angst-filled poetry (see figure 13).

[55] Josh Lange did not have a good reputation amongst the administration. Principal Jenkins called him a "punk and a bully" and said there were "at least a half-dozen times when a student came crying into the counseling office because of some cruel comment that he made." It was also common knowledge that he pressured girls into having sex with him. He had been accused on a number of occasions of sexual assault, but in each case, the girls refused to report the assault to the police.

Stormy's math class.

Stormy shouldn't have listened to Josh. That was a mistake. Because now Chloe is dead and the wrong person is in jail for it.

By the glory of my misery
Autumnal blood streaks my heart
    Shattered dreams replace my pillow
        Hell isn't below ground

Hell is in my skull
    Ebony dreams
        Rust-covered souls

By the glory of my misery
    Razors search for skin
        Always
            Into the darkened corridors
            Nothing nothing nothing
                Screams
.Into another desperate hour
    Night falls

Figure 13: "By the Glory of My Misery." Poem by Stormy Greiner.

PERSON INTERVIEWED: "STORMY" GREINER
DATE OF INTERVIEW: JUNE 23, 2008
TIME OF INTERVIEW: 3:25 P.M.
CASE NUMBER: 06-002050
INTERVIEW CONDUCTED BY: DET. RUSS BUCHANAN
TRANSCRIBED BY: MELISSA HOWELL

BUCHANAN: Tell me more about this Josh Lange. You said you hadn't spoken with him for how long?

STORMY: Oh, man. Years. I mean we had been friends once upon a time, but not in high school.

BUCHANAN: And he approached you? Out of the blue?

STORMY: Pretty much. We were in the hallway. He came up to me and said, "I heard what happened." And then, "Don't worry about it. Nicole is a bitch. She's always been a bitch."

BUCHANAN: How did you respond?

STORMY: I said, "Yeah, I guess she is," and right away I hated myself for saying it. Then Josh said, "You know the difference between a bitch and a slut?" I shook my head, no. "A slut sleeps with everybody," he said. "A bitch sleeps with everybody but you."

BUCHANAN: Seems like a nice guy.

STORMY: He's the worst. I don't know why I ever bothered talking with him. I should have told him to go to hell.

BUCHANAN: But you didn't. And you talked to him again?

STORMY: Yeah. In the cafeteria. This one day I was sitting all alone, eating a sandwich. Josh grabbed me from behind, startled the hell out of me. He said that he wanted to help me out.

BUCHANAN: Wanted to help you out?

STORMY: First, he asked if I had a few minutes to talk. I figured, what the hell. Said, "Go ahead." But he didn't want to talk in the cafeteria. Too many eyes. He asked if we could take a walk.

BUCHANAN: And you agreed?

STORMY: It was a strange request, so I remained sitting for a while. But then I got to my feet and followed after him. I wish I could think for myself more.

BUCHANAN: And where'd you go?

STORMY: The boys' bathroom in the corner of the building. It was empty. Josh kicked the doorstop away so nobody could hear us talking.

BUCHANAN: And?

STORMY: He talked about Nicole for a while. Told me how she was pretty and had a nice little booty. But that she was nothing but a bitch. I told him that I didn't want to talk about her anymore. He kind of laughed, but he agreed. Then he said he wanted to talk about another girl. A girl named Chloe Peterson.

BUCHANAN: And did you know who she was?

STORMY: No, sir. I mean, she was in my English class, but I'd never spoken to her.

BUCHANAN: What did Josh say about her?

STORMY: He said that she was a girl who would put out for me.

BUCHANAN: For you?

STORMY: That's right. Want to know what he said? He said that she'd suck my dick. Let me fuck her from behind. Let me cum on her tits. He said that she was a fucking nympho. Then he told me about all the girls he'd fucked and said that he'd never fucked a girl like her. Called her a freak.

BUCHANAN: And how did you respond?

STORMY: I was uncomfortable. Of course I was uncomfortable. I thought I should leave. But I didn't. I stayed right there. I asked why he was telling me this. And he just smiled and said, "Because I like you, I guess." Then he told me that she had asked about me the other day. Said she thought I was hot. Said she wanted him to set me up with her.

BUCHANAN: And did you believe him?

STORMY: I didn't know what the hell to believe. I mean, I'd never even talked to her. But I guess I wanted to believe it was true. It was kind of flattering, you know. Especially after what had happened with me and Nicole.

BUCHANAN: Understandable.

STORMY: It was all weird. I stood there for a moment and then told him that I appreciated the head's up on Chloe. I said that I would look for her tomorrow. Maybe ask her out for a soda.

BUCHANAN: A soda, huh?

STORMY: Yeah. Josh just laughed at me. Said, "Fuck grabbing a soda." Then he told me the plan. To meet him and Chloe at nine o'clock that night at Hagerman Tunnel over on the Colorado-Midland trail.

BUCHANAN: The same place your sister claimed she saw the Lantern Man.

STORMY: Yeah, sure. But it's also the place where students go to drink, take drugs, or fuck. It's far enough in the woods to prevent cops from patrolling.

BUCHANAN: And you agreed?

STORMY: No. I told him I wasn't interested.

BUCHANAN: And how did he respond?

STORMY: He got pissed. Called me a faggot. Said that Chloe was ready to fuck and what the hell was wrong with me? But I held my ground. Eventually, I got scared and left the restroom. But Josh followed after me. He shoved me against the locker. I stared into his eyes and I knew right then that they were the eyes of a sociopath. "You think you're better than me?" he asked. It was a strange question to ask and I didn't respond. He raised his right arm and I was sure he was going to punch me. But at that moment a teacher walked by. She asked what we were doing. Josh laughed and said that he was just showing me a new wrestling move. She told us to get back to the cafeteria, so that's what we did.

BUCHANAN: And that was the end of the conversation?

STORMY: Almost. On the way back, he apologized for shoving me. Said he shouldn't have done that. Said it was because his dad beats him up. Said his dad used to rape his mom and make him watch. Then he made me promise not to tell anybody about our conversation. Said people might get the wrong idea. Might think that he was gay or something. I agreed.

BUCHANAN: And so? In the following days did you tell anybody about the conversation?

STORMY: Only one person.

BUCHANAN: Who?

STORMY: My sister.

CHAPTER 12

When I was a child, I'd gone to Lakeside Amusement Park in Denver and ridden a roller coaster called the Cyclone. The Cyclone was old and creaky and zipped along a vintage wooden track that seemed on the verge of complete collapse, rattling and shaking with each ascent and descent. I shared a car with Shannon, and while she was giggling with anticipation, I was only terrified as the roller coaster began its slow climb up the tracks, the wheels clicking ominously. I glanced over the side and saw how high in the air we were, the trees and Ferris wheel below, humans resembling moving dolls. And as the roller coaster began its descent, jerking this way and that, as the screams echoed across the park, something strange happened. I felt a powerful urge to wiggle from the seatbelt, rise from my seat, and leap from the ride. If I did this, certainly I would die or, at the very least, be badly maimed. I didn't understand where this urge came from, but it was overwhelming. Not a voice, just a force pushing me to act. For the rest of the ride, I was equally terrified by the thought that I would act on this urge as I was by the sudden drops and jerks of the roller coaster itself. That was the only time I rode that roller coaster.

As I got older, these types of urges became more and more frequent. If my dad were cutting a tree with a chainsaw, I would feel impelled to stick my finger beneath the blade. If I were unclogging a slow drain, I would fight the impulse to take a long chug of Drano. I soon worried that these violent thoughts would lead me to commit a heinous act on somebody else. Turn the chainsaw on another person. Drown a flailing swimmer in the lake. Wrestle a youngster from that childhood roller coaster. Committing such an act would serve no purpose and would bring no satisfaction. But I knew that if I gave into an urge, just a single time, everything would be changed forever.

I think that Stormy felt the same urges. The same forces. The knowledge that once the *possibility* was in his brain, he would have no choice but to act, to hell with the consequences.

That night, the three of us ate dinner, but nobody seemed all that interested in talking. Just silverware clattering on china, food chewed and swallowed.

After eating, Stormy and I helped Mom clear the table and load the dishes. My head was pounding, the start, maybe, of a migraine. I couldn't stop thinking about Stormy's conversation with Josh. The way that asshole talked about Chloe. So crass and dehumanizing. But then, I wasn't all that surprised. That's who Josh was. I'd heard stories about him. About the girls he'd conquered. About the boys he'd destroyed. It was strange that Josh had reached out to Stormy. Stormy wasn't like him. He treated girls well. Thought them worthy of respect. Didn't he?

At some point, sounding suspiciously nonchalant, Stormy said, "I'm gonna head out for the evening if that's all right." As soon as he said it, I felt my stomach tighten.

Mom wiped her hands on a dishtowel and said, "Well, sure, honey. Where are you going?"

He shrugged his shoulders. "Don't know. I'm gonna meet up with a couple of friends. Charlie and Dave. Maybe bowl a game or two. Catch a movie. I shouldn't be home too late."

I opened my mouth as if to say something, but Stormy gave me a look of warning. I didn't say a word.

"Be home by midnight," she said.

"Yeah, sure. Midnight."

Stormy left the kitchen and so did Mom. Then it was just me. I turned toward the window and gazed at my own reflection in the darkened glass. *You ever done something bad and you didn't know why? You ever hurt a person out of spite for the world?*

I looked down at my hands and they were clenched into trembling fists.

Twenty minutes later, I watched from my bedroom window as Stormy stepped outside. The wind was blowing cold, so he pulled up the collar of his leather jacket and shoved his hands into his pockets. From far away the church bells rang. As he walked across the lawn and toward the sidewalk, I pressed my face and hands against the glass, trying to escape my own room. Another minute and Stormy had vanished into the shadows and the quiet.

PERSON INTERVIEWED: "STORMY" GREINER
DATE OF INTERVIEW: JUNE 23, 2008
TIME OF INTERVIEW: 3:25 P.M.
CASE NUMBER:06-002050
INTERVIEW CONDUCTED BY: DET. RUSS BUCHANAN
TRANSCRIBED BY: MELISSA HOWELL

BUCHANAN: You've got to help me understand. Why'd you go to Hagerman Tunnel that night, Stormy? What, exactly, were you hoping for? What did you expect was going to happen?

STORMY: I...I don't know. I've thought about that a lot. I can't say for sure. Maybe I wanted to protect her.

BUCHANAN: Protect who?

STORMY: Chloe. From the world. From Josh. He's a bad person. I figured he might do some bad things. I don't know.

BUCHANAN: Let's talk about that night then. You told your mother that you were going out with friends. But that was never your plan, was it?

STORMY: No.

BUCHANAN: You were going to the hills. Where you expected Chloe and Josh to be.

STORMY: Yes. I guess so.

BUCHANAN: Hagerman Tunnel is quite a ways from your house. Why didn't you drive?

STORMY: I don't have a license. I took the test twice and failed.

BUCHANAN: Okay. Fine. So you walked through town. Walked into the hills. Toward Hagerman Tunnel. It must have been dark. Did you have a flashlight?

STORMY: No. The moon was out and so were the stars. For the most part, I could see just fine.

BUCHANAN: And you passed Opal Lake. Where your sister drowned.

STORMY: Yes.

BUCHANAN: And then finally the tunnel. What time was it when you arrived? Do you remember?

STORMY: I don't know. Maybe nine-thirty? That's just a guess.

BUCHANAN: Okay. And once you got to the tunnel, what did you see?

STORMY: Nothing at first. The clouds covered the moon and it got dark. I didn't think anybody was there. I figured that he'd called the whole thing off. Or he'd been lying the whole time. Honestly, I felt relieved. I was about to turn around. To go home. But then I heard a sound—a low moaning. And then another sound. It sounded like someone was screaming.

BUCHANAN: Screaming?

STORMY: Yes, sir. Instinctively, I held my breath. I tried convincing myself that the sounds were just my imagination.

BUCHANAN: But they weren't.

STORMY: No, sir. The moaning began getting louder. And there was another scream. I took a couple of steps forward, swiping away some branches. And that's when I saw them. It was hard to see, but I saw them. They were on the ridge above the mouth of the tunnel. Two boys and a girl. It took a few moments for my brain to catch up to my senses.

BUCHANAN: Who were they?

STORMY: The girl was Chloe. That I could tell. She was on her hands and knees, naked, her long yellow hair flopping forward and backward. Josh, face half-concealed by the shadows, was kneeling behind her, thrusting in and out, hands gripping her shoulders. The other boy, Billy, stood in front of her, hands folded behind his head, cock bobbing in and out of her mouth.

BUCHANAN: You're talking about Josh Lange and Billy Howard, correct?

STORMY: Yes, sir. I panicked. I dropped to my knees and hid behind some brambles. If I made any noise, they didn't show any signs of having heard. They just continued thrusting, continued fucking. I knew I should close my eyes or look the other way. But I couldn't help myself.

BUCHANAN: How long did you watch?

STORMY: I don't know. Not too long. Josh started to spasm. He grunted, and then his thrusting slowed and finally stopped. A moment later, the other boy, Billy, finished, too. And then they both fell away from the girl and the forest was quiet. I could hear my own breath and worried that they could hear it, too. I had the strange thought that maybe they knew that I was hidden behind the trees and had been performing for my sake. In the moonlight, Chloe was wiping her face with one hand, and wiping her bottom with the other. And then she spoke. Just a single word. "Gross." Can I get a glass of water now?

BUCHANAN: Yes. Yes, of course.

{Break}

BUCHANAN: Okay. Chloe. The boys. Did they see you there? Hidden?

STORMY: No. After they finished, I ducked down lower beneath the bushes and brambles and finally lay on my back. I was scared that they would discover me. What would I say? How could I ever live down being a peeping Tom in the woods? At that moment, my only aim was to not be discovered. I could hear the boys talking and laughing but didn't hear anything from Chloe. I waited there for a long time. The voices and laughter got louder. And then some angry shouting. I couldn't hear what they were saying. Soon I heard footsteps on the dirt and leaves, close to where I was hiding. My heartbeat and breath were too fucking loud. They'd see me, I was sure. But then I heard the footsteps and voices soften and then fade away completely. I wanted to rise and hurry back down the trail, back toward the highway and my house, but I wanted to make sure Chloe and the boys were long gone. So I started counting slowly. All the way to five hundred. Then I waited some more. Other than the winds rushing through the pines, everything was quiet. They were gone. I got to my feet. I started back toward the path. But when I glanced up, I saw Chloe, and she was naked, and she was staring right at me.

BUCHANAN: Just to be clear. The boys had gone. It was only Chloe?

STORMY: That's right. I guess they didn't have any use for her after that.

BUCHANAN: And when she saw you. What did she do? Was she angry? Embarrassed?

STORMY: No. I don't think so. She didn't try hiding or covering her body. She didn't scream or cry. Instead, she took a step forward and nodded her head. She said, "You're that boy from English class." I didn't answer right away. I was surprised she recognized me. I gazed at her naked body. I just couldn't help myself. The truth is, she wasn't very pretty. I don't want to sound mean or anything. I felt ashamed staring at her so I looked away. She took another step forward, and I instinctively moved back. But she wasn't approaching me. She was only retrieving her clothes. She pulled on her underwear and then a T-shirt and a pair of jeans. She pulled her hair out of her face and then placed her hands on her hips. Then she asked why I was here. I didn't know how to answer. "Josh told me," I said automatically. Right away, I wished I hadn't said that. It was a stupid thing to say. She asked me if he'd told me that I could come here and fuck her. I lied and said no. After that, both of us were quiet for a long time. Then she spoke again. She asked if I'd watched her with those boys. I admitted that I had. At least for some of it. I told her that she shouldn't let boys do that to her. She just laughed and said that she liked it. And then she asked me if I wanted to do the same thing to her. I said, "No. Not like that." And she laughed again. It was all wrong. The wind was blowing, rustling the dead leaves and pine needles. She made fun of me. Asked if I was gay or something. I shook my head and told her that I was going to leave. And that's what I did. I turned and ran down the path. I was scared. She shouted something at me, but I couldn't hear her. That was the last time I saw her.

BUCHANAN: You didn't think about walking her home? She was just a girl. There in the forest by herself.

STORMY: You've got to understand. My head was spinning. It all seemed like a dream. Everything was crazy. So, yes, I left. But Chloe was laughing and she was alive. That you've got to know. She was alive.

CHAPTER 13

On the edge of town, directly across the tracks from Mount Massive Liquors and Family Dollar, there stands a small, dilapidated bungalow with blue shutters, concrete steps, and a screen door hanging off its hinges. It is the only residence on the block. This is where Chloe and her mother, Lindsey Peterson, lived.[56]

I imagine that, on this particular night, Lindsey Peterson's old, rusted brown Oldsmobile was parked in the dirt driveway and that Chloe's red bicycle with the bent handlebars lay in the yard. And then add these details: the porch light glowed dully and a pair of dark gray miller moths fluttered spastically around the bulb.

Inside the house, the living room must have been a mess with magazines, clothes, and papers scattered everywhere. What else? The white paint on the walls was bubbling, and the stuffing on the couch was spilling from torn pillows. In the corner of the room, the television was turned to a police procedural, but nobody was there to watch it.

---

[56] It had been a month since Lindsey and Chloe moved from Linden, TX. Lindsey had been in an abusive relationship with Chris Phinney for seven years, but when Phinney put his hands on Chloe—shoved her face against the wall, giving her a bloody nose and a chipped tooth—she finally found the courage to leave. "I figured we'd go to the mountains," she said, "because Chris is a rat and rats burrow not climb. Plus, I thought I remembered having an aunt in Leadville." It turns out, the aunt actually lived in Loveland, not Leadville, about three hours northeast.

114

Walk down the hallway toward the kitchen where an antique refrigerator hummed noisily. Dirty pots and pans and dishes were piled high in the sink and opened bags of bread and lunchmeat and cheese were spread across the counter. In the middle of the room was a small wooden table surrounded by two folding metal chairs. Lindsey Peterson sat at one of them. She was short and fat, hair red, face covered with freckles. A cigarette burned in her hand, the ash lengthening until it finally broke off and fell to the table. In front of her was an empty bottle of wine, and an empty wine glass. Every minute or two she glanced at her watch and sighed. Nearing one o'clock and still no sign of Chloe.

I also imagine that Lindsey Peterson wasn't afraid of hardly anything. Not of snakes or tornadoes or war. Not of fire or water or hell. But there was one thing she was afraid of: losing Chloe. That was the only thing she didn't think she could bear. Well, what mother isn't terrified of that possibility? Every night she would dream of different ways of losing her: a car crash, a disease, an abduction. And she would force herself awake and stumble down the hallway to Chloe's room and peer in there, and each night her daughter would be there, sleeping, body as still as an idol.

But tonight, Chloe wasn't in her room. Tonight, Chloe was missing.[57]

Across town, at the same time Lindsey must have went searching for her daughter, I jerked awake from an awful dream, the

---

[57] Lindsey did not call 911 until the following morning. "I just didn't think they'd be able to do anything," she said. "Also, I was afraid that they'd contact Chris, and I didn't want that to happen." When Chris Phinney was informed that Chloe was missing, he immediately accused Lindsey of being responsible, of maybe even being the one who killed her. He claimed that *she* was the abuser in the relationship, not him. Police photos of Lindsey with a black eye and swollen face contradict his claims. As do similar photos of Sharon Theilke, his ex-wife.

nightmare of slumber quickly replaced by the nightmare of consciousness. I sat up in bed, my sheets damp with sweat. I blinked a few times, eyes adjusting to the darkness. My bedroom door was open, and I noticed a shadowy figure in the hallway. "Who's there?" I whispered, half asleep. "Father, is that you?"

Still half asleep, I rose from bed and tiptoed into the hallway. And now I saw that the figure was my brother and he was moving toward my mother's bedroom. I waited until he disappeared into her room and then I followed after him. He'd left the door open a crack. I stood with my back to the wall and peered inside.[58]

"Stormy?" my mother said, sitting up in bed. "What are you doing? Why are you standing in my bedroom while I sleep? How long have you been there? I had a bad a dream. That usually happens when it's windy. Nightmares are contagious, you know?" She breathed deeply. "Is everything okay? What do you need?"

Stormy shook his head. "I...I need to talk. Can we talk?"

"Of course. Just turn on the lamp. Your sister. Is she asleep? Turn on the lamp."

Stormy took a few steps forward and turned on the lamp. For a moment, my mother shielded her eyes from the glare. Stormy just stood there, rocking back and forth, his eyes gazing at the floor. "What I wanted to say is..."

"Go ahead."

I could tell he was troubled, and it was difficult for him to speak. "I lied to you, Mom. That's what I wanted to say."

"Lied to me?"

"When I told you I was going out to meet friends? I didn't meet friends. I met a girl."

Mom pulled the hair from her face. "It's okay, Stormy. That's not such a terrible thing. I'm not angry. Was the girl Nicole?"

He shook his head. "No, not Nicole. Nicole and I are finished. Her name is Chloe. She's in my English class."

---

[58] The time Stormy entered the room, according to Jessica, was shortly after midnight. She remembers glancing at the clock.

"Okay."

"We met out by Hagerman's Tunnel."

"That's a long walk."

"I could have turned back. A million different times. But instead I just kept walking."

"Has something happened? You're acting strange."

"Her name is Chloe," Stormy said again. "I could have turned back."[59]

Stormy hung his head, and I could see that his shoulders were heaving up and down. Mom rose from bed and walked a few steps toward where Stormy stood. She placed her arm around Stormy's shoulder and pulled him close. He began sobbing, softly at first, but then turning to a mournful moan.

"It's okay. Whatever happened. It's okay."

"I miss Shannon. I miss Dad. I miss him so much."

"Shh. Shh."

"Why'd he have to leave? What's the point?"

"No point. No point at all."

Now Stormy pushed away from Mom, and the way his eyes glowed, he resembled some feral animal. His head cocked and he glanced my way, and I quickly moved my head from view. For a few moments, there was silence and I was sure he'd seen me, but no. He started speaking again. I held my breath and listened. "There's a man," he said. "I see him from time to time on Harrison Avenue. He's got no legs. He's got no arms. He sits in his rusted wheelchair outside the Silver Dollar Saloon. He depends on the kindness of others. Coins echoing in his metal can. An occasional dollar or maybe a five."

"I've seen him, too," Mom said. "He was born that way. That's what I'm told. Life's not always fair."

"He's got no reason to live. None."

"I don't know about that."

---

[59] Jessica Greiner: "He never admitted to laying a hand on her in violence. Never admitted to anything at all. But I had a bad feeling. A mother knows things."

"And yet, he's always smiling. He's always laughing. Why do you think that is?"

"It's hard to say."

"He doesn't understand how terrible he has it. And that makes me sad. That somebody could think he's got a reason to live when he so obviously doesn't. But here's the thing. I don't think any of us do. And some of us smile, too. And some of us laugh. Her name is Chloe. She's just a girl. She's nothing special. I wonder what Dad would say about all of this. I wonder."

And now, once again, he was quiet. I waited, I waited, and still he didn't speak. Shivering, I tiptoed back down the hallway and into my room. I closed the door ever so quietly. For a long time, I sat down on edge of my bed and stared into the darkness. And I thought about the man in the wheelchair. And how he was born that way.[60]

---

[60] On the following pages is my interview with Mrs. Greiner, which expands on her plea-bargained testimony at Stormy's trial.

PERSON INTERVIEWED: JESSICA GREINER
DATE OF INTERVIEW: JUNE 25, 2008
TIME OF INTERVIEW: 9:10 A.M.
CASE NUMBER: 06-002050
INTERVIEW CONDUCTED BY: DET. RUSS BUCHANAN
TRANSCRIBED BY: MELISSA HOWELL

BUCHANAN: So that night. Stormy admitted that he had seen Chloe?

JESSICA: Yes. I wasn't upset that he lied about that. It's something teenagers do.

BUCHANAN: But you said he was acting strange.

JESSICA: He was trembling. His eyes were darting everywhere.

BUCHANAN: And why did you think that was?

JESSICA: I assumed he felt guilty. That he had cheated on Nicole.

BUCHANAN: But weren't they broken up?

JESSICA: Yes. But he still loved her. Still believed they'd get married.

BUCHANAN: And when did you find out that Chloe was missing?

JESSICA: On Monday. It was in the papers. I must have read the article a dozen times. And every damn time, the world became darker. I didn't want to think about it.

BUCHANAN: Think about what?

JESSICA: If he'd had something to do with her disappearance. You need to understand. Stormy has always been so gentle. I didn't think he could ever get mixed up in anything like this. But I wondered if he knew somebody who had.

BUCHANAN: Did you ask him about it?

JESSICA: He was already at school when I saw the newspaper. All day I sat in the kitchen smoking cigarettes and drinking coffee. I figured that I'd talk to him when he got home from school. I felt sick to my stomach. I couldn't get the dark images out of my head. My son and that girl. Him placing his hand over her mouth while she tried to scream.

BUCHANAN: And when Stormy got home?

JESSICA: He and his sister went into the kitchen for a snack. Lizzy was talking nonstop. Stormy was quiet. I waited until Stormy finished his cereal. Then I asked to speak to him in private. We went to Stormy's bedroom. He had left a window wide open, and so the room was freezing cold. He sat down on a wooden chair. I remained standing. There was no good way to start the conversation. I asked him if he'd seen the newspaper article. The one about Chloe. He didn't answer. I asked him again. He just stared straight ahead. Something was wrong with him. He knew something. I was sure of it. I placed my hand on his shoulder. I didn't want it to seem like I was accusing him of anything. I asked him what he knew. Asked him if we needed to go to the police. He just shook his head. And then, eventually, he broke down. He started crying. He told me about those boys. About Josh and Billy. About what he'd seen them do. But he swore he hadn't done anything wrong. I wanted to believe him.

BUCHANAN: What did he say he'd seen them do?

JESSICA: Please, Detective.

BUCHANAN: I only—

JESSICA: They fucked that poor girl. Raped her probably.

BUCHANAN: Is that what he said? That they raped her?

JESSICA: He insinuated it.

BUCHANAN: And he told you that he'd watched? Nothing else?

JESSICA: That's what he said. Eventually, Stormy left the room, still crying. He was a goddamn mess. I stayed there for a long time, trying to decide what to do next. Call the police? Pray? This is my son we're talking about. Eventually, I rose to my feet and walked toward the door. But I had just touched the doorknob when something caught my eye. Crumpled beneath Stormy's bed was a flannel shirt, the same flannel shirt that he'd worn the night he met Chloe. I bent down and pulled it out; then I brought it to my face. I must have stared at that shirt for a minute at least, trying to make sense of things, but no matter how many times I squeezed my eyes shut and then reopened them, I kept seeing the same thing. At the bottom of the shirt, barely visible, were the faded splatters of blood.

BUCHANAN: And you thought that it was Chloe's blood.

JESSICA: I didn't know what the hell to think.

BUCHANAN: Go on.

JESSICA: Well, it was later that night that I made up my mind to visit Hagerman Tunnel. I needed to know.

BUCHANAN: Needed to know what?

JESSICA: It sounds strange, but I thought maybe Chloe would still be there. I wasn't thinking straight. Anyway, I put on my jacket, gloves, and hat. Outside, the snow was falling and the wind was blowing. I got into my truck and drove. It took me ten minutes or so until I got to the parking lot for the trail. It was empty. I opened the glove compartment box and grabbed a flashlight. It took me a while, but I found the trailhead and started walking. The wind was blowing hard. I remember that. And with the flashlight bouncing along the dirt and snow of the trail, everything appeared more menacing. I thought I heard footsteps behind me, thought I heard voices in front of me. But no, just my mind playing tricks on me. There was nobody in the forest, nobody but me.

BUCHANAN: How long did you walk?

JESSICA: I don't know. A while. With the snow blowing in my face, I kept getting disoriented, kept thinking I was off the trail. I'd bend down to the ground and wipe away the snow, make sure the trail was still there. It sounds strange, but the only thing that would calm me down was having conversations with Shannon.

BUCHANAN: Your daughter?

JESSICA: Yes. My dead daughter. I'd say something out loud, like, "It was some stupid decision, to come out here." Then I'd answer. Say what Shannon would say: "Ah, come on. Don't be so hard on yourself. You're just trying to help your son. Besides. The girl, Chloe, is probably fine."

BUCHANAN: Trying to soothe yourself. I understand. And eventually you made it to the tunnel?

JESSICA: Yes. I saw the sign. "Keep out." And then the mouth of the tunnel. Somehow, despite the darkness of the blizzard night, the tunnel seemed illuminated. I pulled myself down the ridge, but as I neared the bottom, the flashlight fell from my hand and disappeared into the snow. On my hands and knees, I crawled forward until I felt the metal handle. I pulled it out and blew off the snow. I noticed that the glass was cracked. It still lit, but with strange shadows. I got to my feet and walked toward the entrance of the tunnel. Actually, it seemed more like a cave than a tunnel, with the way the rocks lay jagged on one another, as if they would collapse at any moment. The floor was all black ice and seemed to be several feet thick. On one of the walls was graffiti, a single word: Monsters. A few beer cans were crushed in the corner.

BUCHANAN: And you walked into that tunnel?

JESSICA: I kept telling myself that Chloe wasn't here. Of course she wasn't here. I kicked one of the beer cans and then took a few steps inside. I called out for Chloe, but, of course, there was no response. And now I started walking slowly, testing each step on the ice before fully committing. After a few steps, I became confident that the floor was thick enough for my full weight. I began to walk a bit quicker, but still cautiously. I breathed deeply. The tunnel smelled of mildew and rot. I called Chloe's name again. I continued walking. The tunnel had been curving without me noticing, and when I spun around I could no longer see the entrance. My flashlight flickered and I thought the light would extinguish, but it remained glowing. Just a few more steps, I decided, and I would turn around. Just a few more steps. And that's when I saw her.

BUCHANAN: Chloe?

JESSICA: She was lying face down, one arm extended, the other flat at her side, as if she were trying to swim across the ice. One of her shoes was on, but the other was missing. I stood there for some time, paralyzed. Then, slowly, I squatted down next to the girl. I placed my hand on her shoulder. I said, "Chloe? Is that you? Chloe?" But I knew it was her, even though I'd never seen her face. And I knew she was dead. I'd always known she was dead. I breathed deeply, trying to remain calm. I reached beneath her and flipped her over. Then I shone the splintered light on her face. The girl's skin was pale blue, her eyes the same. The left side of her skull was caved in. I pulled my own legs to my chest. Then I raised my head to the nobody in the sky and began to cry. I cried for Chloe, a girl I'd never seen before this very moment. I cried for Chloe's mother, standing by the window waiting in vain for her daughter to return. And I cried for my son, the boy who I believed had smashed her skull and left her to die.

BUCHANAN: Did you see anything that might have been used as a weapon?

JESSICA: No. There were rocks, of course. But I wasn't thinking about that. My head was pounding. I stayed on the ground, next to the dead girl, for some time. Eventually I stopped crying and wiped the tears from my skin. Eventually my breath slowed and my heartbeat normalized. Eventually I accepted the new reality. A girl was dead and my son might have killed her.

BUCHANAN: What about the other boys? The ones who had sex with her?

JESSICA: No. It wasn't them. It was Stormy. Just a moment of rage. Everything can change in a moment. Everything.

BUCHANAN: What did you do next?

JESSICA: I took some deep breaths. I knew I needed to think rationally and not worry about morality. I needed to determine the best course of action to protect my son. I'd already lost my daughter, lost my husband. That was all I could bear. You have to understand.

BUCHANAN: I can only imagine.

JESSICA: I decided that it wouldn't do to leave the body in the tunnel. Eventually those boys would talk. They would admit that they brought the girl to Hagerman's Tunnel. The cops would come searching. They would find the body. And then Stormy's name would come up. No, I needed to get the body out of there. I needed to dispose it somewhere far away.

BUCHANAN: And so you moved the body.

JESSICA: That's right. I don't regret what I did. Stormy is a good boy. I reached under Chloe's body and lifted her up. I'm a big woman, and the girl was skinny as a pole, but she wasn't so easy to carry. Her body was stiff, you see. In one hand I held the cracked flashlight. But still it was dark and hard to see. I began walking back toward the entrance of the tunnel and almost laughed at the ridiculousness of the situation. I was an accomplice now. An accomplice to my own son's crime.

BUCHANAN: But you kept going.

JESSICA: Yes. I kept going. It wasn't long until I reached the mouth of the tunnel. The snow was falling even harder than before, and the wind was blowing. The hardest part was getting her up on the ridge. It took all the strength I had. My arms were aching and the trail had all but vanished beneath the thickening snow. With the wind blowing into my face, I felt like a blind woman.

BUCHANAN: And where did you hide the body?

JESSICA: I didn't have a shovel, so I couldn't dig a hole. I thought about burying her beneath the snow but decided that the animals would uncover her far too quickly. I thought about sinking her in the water. Opal Lake wasn't far away. The place my daughter had drowned. But, then I figured they'd drag the water and find her body, her eyes eaten by fish. So I kept walking, and I was to the point of exhaustion. Just take her to the truck, I figured, and drive. A place far from Hagerman Tunnel.

BUCHANAN: And that place was Gilman.

JESSICA: When I was a child, my father used to take me exploring through some of the nearby ghost towns. Carson, Independence, Dearfield, Vicksburg, but the place I remembered most clearly was Gilman. I hadn't been there in a long time, but I figured it would be as good a place as any to bury Chloe, a place nobody would look. I finally made it to my truck. The windshield was thick with frost and snow. Now my arms were throbbing, and I was sweating despite the cold. I managed to get the corpse into the bed of the truck and then covered her with a tarp. I returned to the ground, and now I felt like I was going to be sick. I placed my hands on my knees, and my stomach lurched. For several minutes, I dry-heaved over and over again, and I had a feeling that this was a nausea that couldn't ever be soothed.

BUCHANAN: How far away is Gilman?

JESSICA: I don't know. Twenty minutes? Thirty? It's down Highway 24, a ways. Near Snake River.

BUCHANAN: Been abandoned since the eighties, correct? Toxic.

JESSICA: Yes, sir. It's like stepping back in time a few decades. Most of the houses are still there. Some buildings.

BUCHANAN: So you parked the truck?

JESSICA: Off the highway, there's some winding dirt roads. I drove slowly until I came to the outskirts of town. Then I parked my truck and shut off the engine. I stepped out of the car and slammed the door shut behind me. More nausea, and I grabbed the corpse out of the bed of the truck. Strange the things you remember. I remember all the junk I saw on the way. Mining spoil, washouts, rotted wood. A forced air vent, rotted shack, abandoned car. I was doing this because I loved my son and hated the world. Don't you understand, Detective?

BUCHANAN: I understand.

JESSICA: I walked along the twisted remains of a railroad track. Out of the corner of my eye, I saw the severed leg of a cow protruding from the snow. I remember that. Minutes later, I saw its rib cage and skull, flesh picked clean by scavengers.

Soon I was walking along what once was a neighborhood. Most of the houses were rotted and collapsing to the dirt and snow. Occasionally I saw the worthless remains of a life from long ago: a metal iron, a smashed radio, an ice box. Another ten minutes and finally I came to the place I was looking for, the place I remembered from childhood: the ore processing facility, the spread of buildings collapsing in on themselves. To the side of the last outbuilding, in the ground, was a two-by-three-foot entrance, a metal ladder still securely fastened to the rocks. Both of us wouldn't fit in the narrow entrance, so I placed Chloe's slender body into the opening, feet first, and then released her grip. I listened as she bounced off the sides and eventually hit the ground below. I could have left her there, but I worried explorers or vandals would discover her too quickly, so I followed after, using the broken flashlight to guide my way. I descended the ladder, taking each step gingerly and cautiously, and it seemed that I would never reach the bottom, but eventually my foot hit solid ground and I saw the crumpled and mangled body of Chloe. I waved my flashlight around the stope, the walls lined with dogtooth spar crystals and dripping calcite water. In the corner of the wall, a miner had written "Dec. 3, 1930" with the smoke from a carbide lamp. I grabbed Chloe by the feet and dragged her through the underground tunnel until I came to a side chamber with a scum-covered pond still being fed by seeping water. I shoved the poor girl into the water. She didn't sink, not completely. As I wiped my hands on my filthy jeans, I noticed an old metal sign, half-submerged and pointing toward the bottom of the pool. In faded lettering, it read, "This Way Out."

THE FORENSIC

SCIENCE GROUP

9725 E. Hampden Ave. Ste. #307
Denver, CO 80231
(866) DNA-2969

FORENSIC REPORT

Officer in case:	Det Stephen Kline
Client:	Leadville Police Department
Police reference:	09/08987 Operation TASK
Labaroatory reference	300 667 188
Order reference:	400 912 898
Scientist:	PAM GLADWELL
Number of pages:	2

Re: Homicide of Chloe Peterson on December 8, 2007

A DNA profile has been obtained from the reference samples of Chloe PETERSON (74588898) and Brandon GREINER (74588899).

A DNA profile has also been obtained from a shirt belonging to Brandon GREINER (SJH/1).

In this case, all of the bands present in the profile of the obtained shirt are represented in the profile of Brandon GREINER. This is what I would expect to find if the blood on the shirt originated from him.

The results of the DNA profile obtained from the shirt is approximately 29 million times more likely to be Brandon GREINER's than another individual.

Figure 14: The blood on Stormy's shirt was his own, not Chloe's.

Figure 15: Gilman, CO.

CHAPTER 14

Mom was gone, and I had a good idea where she'd gone.

(*In the pines, in the pines; Where the sun don't ever shine.*)

Maybe it was because I was worried about her and what she'd find, but that night, I couldn't fall asleep, no matter how hard I tried. Every time I began slipping into the abyss, a shock of anxiety would force me awake. And then sounds and whispers and threats. This wasn't so unusual for me because my mind's not right from time to time. One o'clock, two o'clock, three; finally, exhaustion overcame dread. I slipped into another world where the sky was black, the moon and stars vanished behind darkened clouds. I found myself standing alone in Evergreen Cemetery, wearing only the thinnest of nightgowns, a cold breeze causing me to shiver. All around me were headstones and monuments for the forgotten. Crosses made of granite. Black angels made of marble. Death beneath the dirt. Like a ghost, I floated across the grounds until I arrived at a plot that I knew well. I wiped away the grime from the headstone: *Shannon Greiner. October 5, 1990 to July 23, 2007. A daughter, a sister, a friend.* And lying next to the grave, a square-pointed shovel, the wood handle nearly rotted.

Voices whispered in my ear and the rain started falling. With a strange sense of hope, I picked up the shovel and began removing the dirt. The rain fell harder. It seemed that I dug for hours and hours, yet I was making no progress. Then I looked up and saw my father, and he also had a shovel, and he was digging as well. The pile of dirt rose, and the hole got deeper, and then I saw the casket, the same one I'd cried over so many months ago. "Open it," Dad said. And so I pulled open the casket, and now my father was gone, and Shannon was lying there, hands resting on her chest, and she looked so beautiful, just as beautiful as the morning she'd gone missing. I started crying because I missed my sister so much, but then Shannon opened her eyes and her lips spread into a grin, and she said, "Don't cry, Lizzy. I'm alive. I've just been waiting for you to come."[61]

I wiped the tears from my face and said, "I've missed you so much, sister. Why did you have to drown? Why'd you have to leave us here in this mean old world?"

And now I picked up my sister from the coffin, and suddenly I was carrying her through the woods, and the breath was pluming from her mouth. "I'll take you home. And your brother and mother will be there waiting for you. And so will your father. He's missed you as much as anybody."

But instead of a warm house, we entered a blackened tunnel, and Shannon said, "This doesn't look like home. Lizzy, why have you taken me here?" I recognized it as Hagerman Tunnel, and when I looked down I saw that I wasn't holding my sister, I was holding Chloe Peterson, and she was dead, and the Lantern Man had killed her.

The sound of an engine idling woke me. I glanced at the clock: it was nearly four in the morning. I sat up in bed and pulled back the curtain. I could see my mother's truck parked in the

---

[61] According to Dr. Waugh, dreams involving bodily resurrection are not unusual for those who are grieving the loss of a loved one. There have also been several dozen documented cases where a parent or sibling attempted to dig up the grave in hope (or fear) that his or her family member was still alive.

driveway, and I could see that she remained in the cab, her silhouette huddled over the steering wheel, her head bobbing up and down. She sat there for a long time while the snow covered her windshield. Eventually, she got out of the truck, and I thought she was coming inside, but no. Instead, she walked to the back of the house and returned a moment later, a garden hose wrapped around her arm. With a loud grunt, she tossed the hose in the bed of the truck bed and then returned to the back of the house. She must have been trying to turn on the water, but it was December and so the pipes were certainly frozen. Shaking her head and shouting at the wind, she left the hose where it was and shuffled toward the front door. A moment later, I heard the door open and shut. I fell back to the mattress and pulled the blankets over me. How much the world had changed over the past few days, and no amount of scrubbing could rid us of the dirt and blood.

I could hear my mother's shoes creaking in the hallway, and then I could see her shadow outside of my door. A minute passed and the door opened. I squeezed my eyes shut and pretended to be asleep. She stood in the doorway for some time, and I wondered why she was watching me. My eyes opened to slits. The moonlight filtered through the window, casting a pale light and strange shadows. She was a woman broken, my mother, and I was filled with a profound sadness that I knew would always remain. Soon my mother left the room, and then it was just me.

Everybody had to die. Maybe it didn't matter how. Maybe it didn't matter when. Maybe it didn't matter why.

More dreams, all of them terrifying, but I'm sure I was awake when I sensed that there was another body in my bed. I maneuvered until I was facing my brother. "I'm so sorry," he whispered and then pulled the covers over his trembling body. He was only a child, helpless to the machinations of the world. I placed my arm over his chest and held him tightly. I could feel him sobbing, his shoulders heaving up and down. "It's okay," I whispered. "Everything's going to be fine."

It had been a long time since I'd held somebody, and I didn't want to let go. There are so many moments of misery and destruction, but this was a moment of love. And so we lay there, unmoving, as the minutes turned to hours.

"What do you think happened to Chloe?" Stormy asked. "Do you think somebody killed her? And where do you think Mom went in the middle of the night?"[62]

"Just sleep," I said. "Don't worry. I won't let them get you."

For a while, his body relaxed and his breathing slowed. But then, from somewhere, came the muted sound of a siren, and we both stiffened.

---

[62] Jessica never told Stormy what she did with the body, but one night she got drunk and told Lizzy.

CHAPTER 15

For the next several days, it seemed that our house was completely silent. Each one of us held secrets, and some were worse than others. And so, while Mom scrubbed the bed of her truck, Stormy scrubbed the skin of his hands. Meanwhile, I tore pages and pages from my notebook and rewrote my entire story with some truth and more lies, but how can we ever tell the difference?

And so would you accuse me of lying if I told you that one wintry night the Lantern Man himself entered my bedroom? Would you accuse me of psychosis? It doesn't matter. I know what's real.

Remember what my father said: *With black magic, he's able to trap boys and girls in a burlap sack; then he races unseen back to the woods.*

It was late in the evening, and Stormy was talking on the phone (to whom? to whom?) and Mother was in the kitchen, bobbing back and forth, lips slathered in bargain bourbon. Didn't they hear him knocking on the window? Didn't they hear me shouting, "Go away!" No. Mother lovingly took another sip, her tongue probing the inside of the bottle. And Stormy whispered, "But I love you. I'll always love you. My sister is nuts. That's why she's seeing the shrink. That's why..."[63]

---

[63] Stormy did indeed begin speaking with Nicole on the phone, trying to reconcile. We later will learn that this was too much for Lizzy to handle emotionally.

I sat in my bed, cross-legged, staring straight ahead, eyes peeled open in terror.

"Go away," I said, but this time it was only a whisper.

At first the monster had been behind my window, his lantern swinging slightly in the breeze. Then he was inside my room, the lantern in his left hand, the burlap sack in his right. He was whistling that haunted note.

"Go away," but this time it was only a voice in my head.

He moved forward an inch at a time. He'd killed a hundred at least. Don't believe me? Go into his tunnel. Dig beneath the dirt. Now it was my turn.

I could have succumbed. And maybe I should have. But instead, I remembered the story from that encyclopedia, about the woman from Holcomb, Kansas, who struggled from the grasp of the Lantern Man and used his own lantern against him, causing him to shriek in pain and hurry back to the coldness of his tunnel. *And so it is believed that Lantern Men can be wounded, perhaps killed, by fire.*[64]

I had been smart. I kept a torch (a hammer wrapped in cloth) beneath my pillow. I kept a lighter and fuel on my nightstand. My father would have been proud of me. As the Lantern Man got nearer to my bed, whistling that single note, I grabbed the torch and quickly drenched the cloth with fluid. Before the Lantern Man could suffocate me or strangle me, the torch burst into a wild flame. The monster stopped where he was. The whistling ceased. *Fight fire with fire.* The hand of God guiding my every move, I rose from bed and got to my feet. The Lantern Man backed up. I could see his face and it was the face of a dead man.

"I'll burn you," I said. "Just like that woman did."

I moved forward a step and the Lantern Man was screaming silently. "Get him!" my father whispered in my ear, and so I lurched forward. But as I reached toward the ghoul, I lost my footing, and the torch came into contact with the curtain. Just a

---

[64] From The Encyclopedia of Monsters, Ghouls, and Ogres.

single moment, and the fabric turned devilish orange, rising quickly to the top of the window.

The Lantern Man was gone, racing through the woods, but I was paralyzed, watching as the flames become angrier and wilder, the thick smoke quickly filling the room. Within a minute, fire alarms screamed, and now Stormy came charging into the room, panicked, and he held a fire extinguisher in one hand.

"Get out!" he shouted. "Get the hell out!"

But I just stood there, and now Stormy raised the extinguisher and sprayed, the white foam causing the flames to recoil. And as quickly as the fire had started, it became smothered.

My mother, the drunk, appeared in the doorframe. Stormy dropped the extinguisher on the ground and approached me. "What happened?" he asked. "Are you okay?"

Stop talking to that bitch.[65]

"It was him," I said. "I was trying to scare him away."

"Him? Who are you talking about?"

"The one who killed Shannon. The one who killed Chloe. The Lantern Man."[66]

---

[65] Nicole?

[66] "Nobody but Lizzy was there when I got into the room," Stormy said. "She was seeing things, I think. She almost lit the house on fire. But, despite everything, I would never say she was crazy. Maybe the world is crazy instead."

CHAPTER 16

After the fire, I was sure that they hated me. Mom and Stormy both. They thought I was crazy. What was Dr. Urine telling them? I had some ideas. "Yes, indeed. She might be a good candidate for a transorbital lobotomy. I know a man. Very well-regarded."

But I wasn't crazy.

The Lantern Man was real.

Wasn't he?

One thing you should know. My mother was a goddamn drunk. And you know what happens when you're a goddamn drunk? You start telling your daughter things you shouldn't tell them. You tell her how you found a young girl's body, a girl named Chloe Peterson, in Hagerman Tunnel. You tell her that when you found her it looked like she was swimming across the ice, one shoe on, one shoe off. You tell her that her skull was caved-in and her eyes were open, forever staring at the terrors of death. And you know what else you tell her? You tell her that it was your own brother who killed her. "Oh, Lord. Can you picture it, Lizzy? Stormy, face red with fury, raising a rock high in the air and then coming down hard. A murderer! A murderer!"[67]

I didn't correct her because she never would have believed me.

---

[67] Forensics believes that the murderer held her to the ground and attempted to strangle her before crashing her skull with the rock.

It wasn't Stormy.

The very next night, Mom sat at the kitchen table, peeling a carrot down to the nub while Stormy stared out the window at the darkness. What was he thinking about? Damnation? Redemption? Fool! Redemption isn't offered to the likes of us.

I needed to get out of the house. I couldn't bear to be in that stifling environment for another second. It wasn't just them. Old sounds and sights from my childhood were returning. Remember the bloody baby, trapped in the attic? Remember the preacher in the bowler's hat? They were all there. I rose from the table, and Mom and Stormy both turned their glares toward me. "Leaving," I muttered. Staggering, even though I hadn't touched a drop of Mom's booze, I entered the living room and grabbed my jacket off the back of the couch. I stepped outside into the night, the snow falling slantways and turning more and more angry.

And so I walked. It seemed that nobody else was out tonight; perhaps everybody was already hibernating for the winter months, which seemed to last forever. I knew where I was walking, but I didn't know why I was going there.

About twenty minutes later, I stood in front of her little blue bungalow. Lights glowed dully from behind the blinds. I remained there, staring at the house, my stomach tightening. I reached into my jacket pocket and pulled out a package of my mother's Salem Lights. I lit a cigarette and sucked down the smoke, my eyes narrowing into slits. A radio was playing somewhere. Something by Tammy Wynette. Or maybe there was no music at all.

Another few minutes and I tossed the cigarette aside. Snow crunching beneath my feet, I walked slowly across the railroad tracks and toward the house. The screen door hung off its hinges, and I moved it aside and rapped on the door. Then I took a step back. Less than thirty seconds and the porch light shined on and the door opened. Lindsey Peterson stood there, a cigarette (also Salem Lights?) dangling from her fingers.

For a long moment, the two of us stood there, staring at each other, and I felt like I was staring into my own soul. So much loss. Then Lindsey spoke, her voice harsh. "Who are you? What do you want?"

My mouth opened but no words came out. Why was I here? It made no sense. I should have turned around and left. That's what I should have done. It was all just a misunderstanding. I had the wrong address. But, no. Instead, I said, "I've read about your daughter. I'm sorry. I'm so sorry. My sister died last year. I thought we could talk. I don't know."

Lindsey placed the cigarette to her mouth and sucked down a fistful of smoke. She didn't move an inch, and she didn't say a word. The snow continued falling, turning my hair white and wet. This was all a mistake. I said, "I'm sorry. I'll leave you alone."

I turned and started toward the street. But then Lindsey said, "Wait." I stopped and turned back around. She took another drag of her cigarette and then dropped it on the porch and crushed it out with her foot. "Come inside if you want," she said.

A moment's pause, and then I nodded my head and returned to the porch and then went inside. In her living room, the furnace was groaning, and it was very hot. Chloe's backpack lay in the corner of the room. Lindsey nodded at a couch, stuffing visible through torn fabric, and I sat down.

She cleared her throat. "Do you want something to drink?"

"I could use a beer," I said.

She smiled. "I don't think you're old enough."

"Maybe not. But I could still use one."

"Fine," she said. "You want a beer? I'll get you a beer. They want to arrest me, that's okay with me."

Lindsey disappeared into the kitchen. She called out, "I'm not used to the snow. I'm from Texas. I can't say I like it much. I can't say I like Leadville much."

Then she returned to the living room and handed me the beer. I cracked mine open and took a small sip. Lindsey unfolded a plastic lawn chair and sat down. She took a much larger gulp.

"So your sister died, huh?" It was spoken with less empathy than I expected.

"That's right. Her name was Shannon."

Lindsey reached into the pocket of her flannel and pulled out another cigarette. She placed it in her mouth but didn't light it. "It's too bad." Then, "Want a cigarette? I mean, why stop with one bad habit?"

"Yes. Please."

Lindsey stuck a second cigarette in her mouth and lit both of them. Then she walked across the room and handed me one of them. For the next few minutes, the two of us sat in silence, drinking beer and smoking cigarettes. Outside, a train whistle moaned. It was nice.

"Your sister. How'd she die?" Lindsey finally asked.

I took another swallow of beer and another puff of tobacco. "She drowned."

"Hmm."

"She was with my brother and me. We tried saving her. But we didn't."

"And that must be tough for you. Wracked with guilt."

"Yes. It is. I can't sleep at night."

The phone rang, startling us both. Always a glimmer of hope, so Lindsey jumped to her feet and hurried across the room where an old-fashioned phone was bolted to the wall. She picked up the receiver and said, "Yes?" Then she turned her back toward me, and I couldn't hear what she was saying. After a few minutes of conversation, she hung up the phone. She remained standing there for some time before turning around. She wiped a tear from the corner of her eye and returned to her chair.

"About your daughter?" I asked.

Lindsey shook her head. "Sort of. I had a boyfriend. A real asshole. They thought that maybe he would know something. It took them a while, but they finally found him."

"Yes?"

"And he was still in Texas. And he was drunk. But he didn't have my daughter."[68]

More silence. There was too much pain in the world. Too much madness and devastation of souls. Nothing left to do but wait patiently to perish.

"My brother," I said, "knows your daughter." I almost said "knew" your daughter. How painful the past tense could be.

Lindsey looked up and then quickly back down again. She took a drag from her cigarette and then let it burn above her lap. "Is that right? How does he know her?"

"They have class together. English, I think. He's worried about her, of course. Everybody is. He said that she's nice. Quiet. Smart." I didn't know why I was making things up. But it felt right.

"Yes. She is quiet. And she is nice. She hasn't had it easy, you know? I guess nobody does."

And it was at that moment that I felt an overwhelming bond for Lindsey. Maybe it was even love. Only two people who had lost so much could share this love. I hated myself for thinking it, but in a way I was glad that Chloe wouldn't be coming back. Because I needed Lindsey's love as much as Lindsey needed mine.

While my cigarette melted to an ember and my empty beer can lay crushed on the floor, I rose from the couch and moved across the room to where Lindsey sat in her beach chair. I stood next to her and, with a spurt of courage, began stroking her hair and rubbing her back.

The physical contact seemed to move something in Lindsey, and she gasped back a mournful sob.

"It's okay," I said. "You can cry. You can let it all out. Tears are good for you. I'm here for you. For every minute."

The tears came hard and fast. She placed her hands on her knees and cried and cried. I rubbed her back and shoulders and

---

[68] Lindsey has since moved back to Texas and is again living with Chris Phinney.

told her everything was going to be okay.

"My baby," Lindsey sobbed. "She left me and she isn't coming home."

"There, there."

"I'll never kiss her forehead. I'll never hold her tight. I'll never tell her I love you. She isn't coming home."[69]

---

[69] As far as I can tell, this meeting never happened. I don't believe, in fact, that Lindsey and Lizzy ever spoke. However, in Lindsey's house there happens to be a couch with the stuffing visible through torn fabric. She happens to smoke Salem Lights and drink Olympia beer. Question: how would Lizzy know those details? It is conceivable that she spent some time in the Peterson house as well—a habitual Goldilocks.

CHAPTER 17

Lindsey was right. Chloe never did come home. But at least there were some developments in the investigation. Some sense of the players involved. And it was all because Josh Lange liked to brag.

The truth is, he never stopped bragging. About how many tackles he'd made in a game. About how many colleges were recruiting him. About how many girls he'd banged. So it shouldn't have been much of a surprise that the day after the fateful meeting at Hagerman Tunnel, he bragged to anybody who would listen about what he and Billy had done. Yes, he told six or seven of his best buddies. The type of non-puritanical guys (and a couple of gals) who would appreciate his exploits. And word spreads quickly. Especially in high school. "I took her up to the hills," he said. "Fucked the shit out of her. She was like a dog in heat."[70]

But once Chloe's face appeared on the front page of the local paper, a few of those buddies got to thinking. Maybe she'd been so ashamed at what she'd done that she'd run away. Maybe she'd gone and killed herself. Or maybe it was something more sinister.

---

[70] Among the people he told: Gary Watkins, Sean Phillips, Ted Prentiss, Ian Buchannan, Wyatt Howard, Zack Holcomb, and Davey Thompson. While it is true that he and Billy were both suspects, his public braggadocio cast doubt that he played a role in the killing.

I heard that it was Gary Watkins, the boy with the cauli-flower ears, who finally told the cops about Josh and Billy.[71] Once that happened, I knew that it was the beginning of the end. I knew that pretty soon it would come out that Josh had told Stormy about the meeting, and that pretty soon they'd figure out that Stormy had been at the tunnel as well. And then what? I'd seen enough movies to know the process. They'd lock him in an interrogation room. They'd deprive him of legal advice. They'd threaten and manipulate. And eventually he'd confess to a crime he didn't commit.

The way I looked at things, I didn't have much more time with him. I wanted to hold on to each and every moment.[72]

It was during those days that Stormy and I hid in my bedroom, away from the fire and destruction of the world. We played board games like Battleship and Risk and Monopoly. We sang karaoke. We munched on Oreo cookies. And, of course, we laughed a lot. It seemed like it had been a long time since we'd laughed together. Maybe since Shannon had died. Mom wasn't a part of the laughter. She remained in the living room, drinking booze and watching bad TV. And Nicole? I didn't think about her much, but I bet she thought about us. I bet that during those moments she was standing across the street, staring at our window, wondering what we were doing. I bet. I remembered what Stormy had told me about her. *She's nice, but she's just a girl. You don't have to worry about her. I promise that you'll always be my number one.*

So we played games and laughed. I won a couple times, but most of the time I let him win. I wanted him to stay happy. Eventually we both got bored with rolling dice, so we sat on my

---

[71] It was actually Ted Prentiss who, after learning of her disappearance, told his father about Josh's boasts. Mr. Prentiss called the police the same day.
[72] Josh did tell Detective Kline about his conversation with Stormy but, interestingly, Detective Kline did not immediately interview Stormy.

bed and talked. It was nice. For a while, there was no talk of Nicole or Chloe or murder investigations. Only happy conversations. I asked him what he was going to do after high school, what kind of a difference he was going to make, and he squeezed his eyes shut and nodded his head for a few moments. Then he opened his eyes and smiled kind of slyly. He said, "I don't know exactly, Squirt. I just know one thing. I know I'm going to get the hell off this mountain. That I promise you. The day I toss that graduation hat in the air, I'll be gone. Maybe I'll become a cop or a firefighter. Or maybe I'll get an easy job working in a bank. But whatever I do, it'll be far from here, far from this sad luck town. I won't be burrowing underground like Dad and his dad and his dad. That's for damn sure. There's no happiness in mining. No happiness at all."

I nodded my head in agreement. I liked his idea. Going far away. But it would have to be somewhere warm. Like Florida or California or Hawaii. "What about a girl?" I asked, and I don't know why. "You gonna find a girl and marry her? Have a couple of kids?"

He looked at me kind of funny and then he forced a smile. "I don't know," he said. "Maybe. How the hell should I know?" *I promise that you'll always be my number one.*

After that, neither of us talked for a long time. I could hear the sound of the laugh track echoing in the living room. Every few seconds, another burst of laughter. It was unnerving.

Time passed, and I could hear Stormy breathing. When he finally spoke again, his voice sounded strange, like an old man's. He said, "It's just that...I wish things were different."

"Different? What do you mean?"

And now he started rocking back and forth, shaking his head. Then he covered his face with his hands. He said, "I wish they didn't keep dying. All those girls."

It was an odd thing to say. It wasn't his fault that they kept dying. And I told him so. I said, "You didn't do anything wrong, Stormy. I know you didn't."

He pulled his hands away from his face and turned toward me. I could see that his eyes were red and beginning to tear up. "No," he said. "I've done a lot wrong. You might not know about it. But God knows. And the day of reckoning will come."

"God doesn't know. He stays out of Leadville."

And now I placed my head on his shoulder. I loved him so much. Outside the snow fell. The long winter was coming, and poor Stormy would have nobody to hold.

He stared at his hands. "Sometimes...when I'm sitting alone in the darkness...and the snow is falling in such a way...I begin imagining that I...that I..."

"That you what, Stormy? What are trying to say?"

I could feel his shoulders heaving. The poor boy was crying. "That I killed her. That I took a rock and bashed in her skull. That's what I imagine. And I can't get the image to go away. It seems that the harder I try, the more relentless that image is."

"Stormy, oh, Stormy."

"And maybe it doesn't matter if I killed her or didn't kill her. Just that I have the capacity. That we all have the capacity."

"No. That's wrong, Stormy. You know that's wrong. You could never do something like that. Not in a million years. You could think about it. Talk about it. But you could never do it. I know you well enough to know that."[73]

"Maybe," he said. "Maybe."

"Your heart is only filled with goodness," I said.

He turned away from me because he didn't want me to see him crying. He didn't want to look weak.

I reached around and touched Stormy's smooth cheek with the back of my hand. "I'm sorry that I messed things up with you and Nicole."

He nodded his head a few times. "It's okay. I forgive you."

---

[73] Nicole McKenna: "I know he didn't do it. With every ounce of my being, I know he didn't do it."
Jessica Greiner: "I can't say one way or another. I think anybody is capable of anything. That's what I think."

"What do we do now?" I asked. "Everything is upside down."

Stormy didn't speak for a long moment. For some reason, my heart was pounding. Everything else was quiet, and I worried that he would hear it beating. Now Stormy spoke in a whisper. He said, "Sometimes I wonder if I can bring back Shannon. I wonder if I can bring back Chloe. Maybe. Maybe. Maybe."

Maybe.

And then I did something unexpected. I didn't plan it out or anything. It wasn't something that I'd thought of doing. I leaned forward and kissed him—not on the lips but on the corner of his mouth. I shouldn't have done that, and I felt ashamed right away. Our eyes met, for just a moment, and then Stormy pushed me away. "What are you doing?" he said, and it was all wrong.

"Nothing. I just thought that—"

"You can't do that, Lizzy," he said. "You can't." He could hear my heartbeat. Damnit. He pulled his body out of my bed, toppled to the floor, and staggered out of the room, kicking closed the door behind him.

Goodbye, Stormy, goodbye.

After he left, I stayed in bed for a long time, my lower lip quivering, tears streaming down my dirty cheeks. It was no use, I decided. I ruined everything I did. Eventually, I rose from the bed and walked across the room. I pulled the curtain back from the window and stared at the snow falling on the darkened yard outside. And there was the Lantern Man, standing on the edge of the property, his flame extinguished by the cruel wind. "The world," I whispered, "is sad and terrifying. I'll be seeing you soon, Shannon."[74]

---

[74] While this statement is troubling, I am convinced that Lizzy did not commit suicide.

CHAPTER 18

A week and two days later the world died. I didn't see Stormy kiss Nicole, press his skin against hers, but I knew. As soon as he walked into the door, shortly after eleven, I knew. Maybe it was the goofy grin on his face. Maybe it was the hint of adolescent perfume. Maybe it was his ruffled flannel shirt. Or maybe it was just an innate understanding of my brother's obsessiveness and weakness.[75]

He acted like nothing had happened. With a too-cheerful voice, he said, "Hey, Squirt," and then tried embracing me, but I shrunk away.

"You've been gone a long time," I said, and it was less of an observation, and more of an accusation.

"Yeah. I know. I was just out walking. I was feeling kind of sad. You know how it goes. I sat in front of Shannon's grave for a while. I miss her."

I felt a sudden burst of rage. "Why didn't you just dig her up, if you miss her so much?" I said. "She probably looks just fine. It takes years for a body to decompose, you know."[76]

---

[75] Lizzy was right. Stormy and Nicole had reconciled. She saw this as a betrayal. It is around this time, then, that she made the decision to write the letter implicating Stormy.

[76] In ordinary soil, with no coffin, an unembalmed corpse takes up to twelve years to decompose. If the body is sealed in a strong coffin, it can take many years longer.

Stormy grimaced and groaned. "Ah, Jesus, Lizzy. Why do you have to say things like that?"

A shrug of the shoulders. "Don't know. I guess I was born bad. Just like you and Shannon were born good."

"Damn it, Lizzy. Knock it off."

But I didn't want to knock it off. "It's too bad we killed Shannon," I said, and my voice didn't sound like my own.

"Stop that," Stormy said. "Just stop that. Why would—"

"Remember her flapping all about? Gasping for air?"

"Don't do this—"

"And we were so fucking clueless. Just swam right past her. Let her die."

"I don't want to listen to this."

I sort of laughed, sort of snorted. "Okay, fine," I said. "What should we talk about? Want to talk about tonight? Want to tell me where you were? Oh, but I think I know. I think you were with Nicole. Am I right? Is that where you were so late?"

Stormy watched me for a long time, the way a psychiatrist would watch his patient. *I'm not crazy.* Then he nodded his head. "Yes. I was with Nicole again. I wanted to be with her. We're trying to make it work again."

More snorting and laughing. "Trying to make it work?"

"Yes. That's right. Do you have a problem with that? Because—"

"No problem at all. Only it's not going to work. Because she's a little bitch. She'll cut out your heart from your chest and stomp on it with her foot. Maybe spit on it a time or two. Is that what you want? And while you're staggering through the woods, life draining from your veins, she'll watch you from a distance and laugh and laugh and laugh."

If Stormy was affected by my hurtful language, he didn't show it. His expression remained stoical. "I'm sorry you feel that way. I don't know why you're filled with such hatred. I don't know why you're filled with such violence. Nicole never did anything to you. Why do you dislike her so much? Why do you want me to be miserable?"

I quickly shook my head. "No. You've got it all wrong. I don't want you to be miserable. I want you to be happy. That's why I hate Nicole. Because she's just like all of those girls. She's going to make you cry. Maybe worse."

"Okay, fine. I appreciate your concern. But I'm an adult now. I can figure things out on my own."

"I never said you couldn't."

He glanced over my shoulder. "Where's Mom?"

"I don't know. She's gone, too. I've been by myself. It's fine. That's how I want to die."

And now Stormy grinned. "C'mon, Sis. You're being a little dramatic, don't you think? A little morose?"

"Yeah. Dramatic. That's it. I think I'll go to bed. I hope you and Nicole make it work. I hope she likes you. I know that Chloe did."

"What did you say?" And now the stoicism was gone and Stormy grabbed me by the arm.

I laughed a cruel laugh. "You don't think I know?"

"Know what? What the fuck are you talking about? Come on. Spit it out."[77]

"I'm going to bed. Let go of my arm."

"Know what? You think I had something to do with her disappearance? Is that it? Come on. Say something."

But I wouldn't answer. Instead, I marched down the hallway and slammed shut and locked my door. Stormy pounded on it a few times, called out my name, but I ignored him. Eventually, he gave up and left me alone.

As I stood there, I couldn't help thinking how Chloe and Stormy would've been an awfully nice pair.

---

[77] Some of the most damning evidence against Stormy was his own family's reluctance to defend him. He was essentially abandoned in the courtroom.

A few minutes later, I sat on the floor and pulled out my special cigar box. I opened it up and stared at the contents. First, an antique key, a silver one with a snake-like K filling the oval opening. I'd found it years ago buried beneath the dirt at the Ice Palace Park. At the time, I wondered if a prisoner was trapped somewhere while I held the key to his freedom. Then my Reggie Jackson baseball card. In the photograph, he'd just completed a mighty swing and his body was twisted into a near pretzel. Dad had given me that card. He was a Yankees fan and said he was the greatest slugger he'd ever seen. Some silver from the Matchless Mine. And finally, my sister's necklace. Ah, hell. It was really just a worthless brass chain with a little heart medallion connected. Shannon had bought it at the Family Dollar shop and had worn it just about every day. No, that's wrong. Actually, she'd bought two of them and given one to me. After all, we had matching faces. We needed to have matching necklaces. It was nice of her. But one day, out of boredom and unexplained resentment, I unsnapped the chain and tossed it in the river. When Shannon asked where the necklace was, I said the chain had broken and I didn't know where the necklace was and I was so, so sorry. But Shannon didn't make me feel bad. Instead she gave me her necklace. "That way you can think of me when we're not together," she said. Now I placed the necklace against my lips and I so badly wanted to cry, but I had no tears left, not a single one.

"I miss you so much, Shannon," I said out loud. "We were happy, weren't we? I think so. It was just the three of us, and that was all we needed."

I squeezed my eyes shut and huddled into the fetal position. I had nothing more to give. Nothing more to take. I held the necklace, and now maybe the tears were finally coming.

"Yes, it was just me, you, and Stormy. But then that all changed. Then you were pulled into the lake and your mouth was filled with water. Oh, Shannon. Did you do it on purpose? Did you? Did you want to abandon us? Abandon the world? Is that what happened? Or was it something else? Was it the Lantern Man? Was he the one? Yes, yes. That's what happened, I think. I'm sure of it."

Now my voice was just a whisper, but still I spoke because I had to. "Something you should know. When you left me, when you left us, I thought I could survive. Because even though you were gone, I still had Stormy. No longer the three of us, but now the two of us. I thought I could survive. And maybe I could have if Stormy had been true. If he had reentered the womb with me. But no, but no. He left me, Shannon. Abandoned me. Just like everybody. I should have known. The two of us were monozygotic. Same face. Same eyes. Same soul. But not Stormy. He was a singleton. He was never like us. Never. We pretended that he was. But he was different. He wasn't us."[78]

And now the questions I couldn't stop asking. "What do you think should happen to him, Shannon? How do you think he should be punished? And also, what do you think should happen to me? How do you think I should be punished?"[79]

---

[78] As I've already made clear, Lizzy and Shannon were twins. They were not triplets.

[79] This is the punishment Lizzy decided upon: On January 3rd, she sat down in her room and wrote a letter. It detailed what she knew about the death of Chloe Peterson. Six days later, she mailed it. A jury member, Samantha Garcia, was quoted as saying, "It was the letter. That's what convinced me. His sister confessed for him."

Figure 16: Photos of some of the items Lizzy referenced from her cigar box.

January 3, 2008

To Whom It May Concern:

What you should know. I love my brother. I love my mother. I don't want to do them harm. I don't want to do anybody harm. But there are some things you should know.

   That girl Chloe Peterson is dead. It's such a shame. You'll need to tell her mother. It's the worst news a mother can receive. She'll never stop crying probably. Her body is in Gilman, the ghost town. It's a scary place and the air is poisoned. Here's how to find her. Down on the edge of town there is an old ore processing facility. To the side of the last outbuilding, in the ground, is a 2-by-3-foot entrance, a metal ladder still securely fastened to the rocks. Go down the ladder and there's an underground tunnel. Follow the tunnel until you come to a side chamber with a scum-covered pond. That's where Chloe is. It's an awful resting place, so I hope you can give her a proper burial. My mother, Jessica Greiner, was the one who took her there. She got drunk one night and she told me everything. She only wanted to protect her son. You can't blame her. She had nothing to do with her death, however. Spare her punishment.

   The truth: Stormy is a good boy. He's got a good heart. When I broke my arm, he carried me in his arms, a mile or two at least, to our house. How many brothers would do that? Just like Mom always tried protecting him, he always tried protecting me. It was one mistake he made. One moment. How many moments are there in a lifetime? Hundreds of millions. And it was just a single moment. Have mercy on him. Have mercy on his soul.

He didn't know Chloe well. In fact, it was the first time he'd ever spoken to her. It was that boy, Josh, who convinced him to come to the mountains. Said that Chloe wanted to fuck him. He never should have gone. A single moment. He was broken-hearted because Nicole had released him back into the river. And so he approached her. So he kissed her.

She could have kissed him back. Then she'd be alive. But she didn't. She pushed him away. She humiliated him. Here's the thing. She'd already fucked those other two boys. Stormy just wanted to kiss her. He didn't want to fuck her. He's a good boy. She said some things. They were nasty. She was egging him on. He should have walked away. He should have gone home. I was waiting at home for him. We could have hidden under the blankets. We could have slept until noon. But he didn't go home. He got angry. He hit her. And then he hit her again. And then he picked up a rock.

I wasn't there. This is only what I heard. What I suspect. He might be innocent. He might be. This is only what I heard. My mother got drunk. She can't keep her fucking mouth shut.

My mother only wanted to protect her son. My brother only wanted to protect his sister. But me? I'm only protecting my soul.

He might be innocent. We all might be innocent.

I'm so fucking sorry.

Lizzy Greiner

CHAPTER 19

The three of us sat in the living room. I was writing and drawing. Pictures of the Lantern Man. Stories of possible redemption. My mother was pretending to drink iced tea, but I knew what was inside. I can't blame her. It was only because of her insomnia. Just an hour of sleep and she could function. But without it, the world would become darker and darker, a shroud thrown over the sun. Meanwhile, Stormy was sitting on the couch, staring at his hands. There is no way to scrub blood that can't be seen. We have learned that from life and literature. Remember Lady Macbeth walking and talking in her sleep, all the while rubbing her hands together? "What, will these hands ne'er be clean?" she asks, and then, "Here's the smell of the blood still: all the perfumes of Arabia will not sweeten this little hand." Or from Isaiah: "For your hands are defiled with blood, and your fingers with iniquity."

A myth that Jesus died for our sins. We keep committing them, and the blood keeps getting thicker and thicker on our skin. He only died for the sins of one, not all. Picture my mother on her hands and knees, inside of Hagerman Tunnel, scrubbing the floor clean. The water in her bucket has turned bright red and she will be there all winter until her fingers stiffen from the cold and her mouth freezes in an eternal scream. See Stormy, too, with that pointed shovel, digging all the dirt that he can, hoping he'll find a body that he can resurrect. And then me, following behind the Lantern Man, perhaps a wide-eyed apprentice.

There was knocking on the door. Three loud knocks. Followed by a pause. Then three more knocks. Mother opened her eyes and blinked a few times. She looked at the glass of booze on her lap and the cigarette burning in the ash tray. She didn't make any move to rise to her feet. Because she knew. We all knew.

Stormy continued staring at his hands. "Out, damned spot!" Was he thinking about kissing Nicole? Was he thinking about kissing Chloe? A kiss can have a million different meanings. And now the knocking. There was no need to hurry. They wouldn't leave. They would knock forever if they needed to.

I finished the final touches on my latest drawing. The Lantern Man carrying a girl (was it Chloe? was it Shannon? was it me?) into the tunnel. And all the bodies of other girls, missing. A collector of souls. That's what he was. We all end up there, eventually. In that blackened tunnel. Knock, knock, knock.

And now we all rose in unison. We all walked slowly forward. It was me who opened the door. Had I really written that letter? Had I really mailed it? No, it was just a dream. They'd figured it out on their own. They didn't need my help. They'd found footprints at the scene of the crime. DNA on the body. They'd talked to witnesses who placed Stormy at the scene of the crime. No, I'd never mailed the letter. Sure, I'd been angry at Stormy. But not angry enough to condemn him to a cell. It was just a dream.[80]

Yes, it was me who opened the door. Standing on the other side of the screen door were two men. I figured there would be more. One of them had red hair and looked very young. Too young to be a police officer, it seemed. The other was short and fat with a ridiculous black mustache. Did he dye his mustache? He must have to make it that dark. I recognized him from somewhere, but didn't know from where. These were the men

---

[80] This was an argument made by the defense—that the letter hadn't actually been written by Lizzy and had instead been written by some unknown person attempting to frame Stormy. Under cross-examination, however, Lizzy tearfully admitted that it had indeed been her who'd written those words of condemnation.

who would take Stormy away. They had done a thorough investigation. They had interviewed dozens of witnesses. They wouldn't pay attention to a silly letter written by a silly girl. Especially one who told so many stories.[81]

The fat cop nodded his head and flashed his badge. I would confess to the crime! That's what I'd do! And then Stormy wouldn't have to go to jail. It wouldn't be so bad for me. With good behavior, I'd be out in no time. But, no. I didn't confess.[82] I was a coward. "We're looking for Brandon Greiner," the officer said. "Our understanding is that he lives at this address."

Stormy remained where he was, rocking back and forth, an asylum mute. Mom stepped forward. Now she was the mama bear. "What's this all about?" she said. "What do you need Stormy for?"

"Ma'am," the fat cop said. "These things are never easy."

"What do you need him for? He hasn't done anything wrong. Not now. Not ever."

And now Stormy stopped rocking and spoke. His voice sounded small. "I'm Brandon," he said. "But everybody calls me Stormy."

The two officers entered. They hadn't been invited. The fat one did all the speaking. Yes, his mustache was definitely dyed.

He tipped his cap upward and nodded at Stormy. "Brandon Greiner. You're under arrest for the murder of Chloe Peterson."

Now the baby-faced officer removed his handcuffs and placed them on Stormy. He was a good boy and didn't deserve this kind of treatment. I had never sent the letter. I'd thrown it in

---

[81] At the scene of the crime (as well as the final body location), there were no usable footprints. There was no conclusive DNA. And the only witness who mentioned Stormy in relation to the crime was Josh (hardly a reliable witness at that). So, yes, they paid attention to the "silly letter written by a silly girl."

[82] In Bedau and Radelet's 1987 study, false confessions were the third leading cause of wrongful conviction; In Warden's 2003 study they were the single leading cause. He determined that 63% of false confessors were under the age of 25, and 32% were under 18.

the garbage. I'd been mad, but I hadn't sent the letter. Was it possible that somebody had dug out the letter and mailed it to the police department? It wasn't my fault. What is truth?

"You have the right to remain silent," the fat cop said. "Anything you say can and will be used against you in a court of law. You have the right to an attorney. If you cannot afford an attorney, one will be provided for you. Do you understand the rights I have just read to you?"

Stormy nodded his head. "I understand," he said.

He was calm, as always. But Mother wasn't. She'd already lost too much. Even Job couldn't remain passive forever. And so it was that she gnashed her teeth and yanked at her hair. Then tried separating her son from the arresting officer. She yanked at his arms, slapped at his chest, and then started hitting him on his upper back and head. The freckled cop moved toward his sidearm, but the fat cop told him to remain calm. He said, "Ma'am, I need you to move away. Do you hear me? Move away or we'll be forced to arrest you as well."

Finally heeding his advice, Mom backed away from Stormy and the officer. Stormy forced and smile and said, "It's okay, Mom. It's okay, Lizzy. I didn't kill that girl. It's okay. Justice always prevails."

Justice always prevails.

The officer tugged at Stormy's arm and they walked toward the front door. Mom fell to her knees and began sobbing mournfully. "Why? Why? Why?" Meanwhile, I remained where I was, unmoving. Ever since the officers had entered the house I had been stricken by a kind of paralysis. Maybe I had mailed the letter, after all. Maybe I had condemned my brother to something worse than death. I couldn't move. It wasn't until long after the door had shut that I was finally able to drag my body across the room. I stood at the window. And now I saw him standing in front of the police car and his body was turned toward the house. I pressed my face and my hands against the window. Stormy saw me and nodded his head stoically. Then they pushed his head down, and he disappeared into the car. For several minutes the car didn't move, and I wondered if they had changed their minds and were going to release him back into the world. But, no. The car drove slowly down the block before turning at Harrison Avenue, and I worried that I would never see him again.

I remained at the window for some time. I remained there as my mother cried and prayed, eventually vomiting her misery onto the hardwood floor. I remained there as the afternoon light faded and the shadows of nighttime filled the sky. Stormy was gone and I'd been the one who condemned him. What would my punishment be?[83]

Mom spent the rest of the evening on the telephone, calling anybody who might have an idea of what they could do to get Stormy out of jail, but they all agreed that it was best to let the lawyer handle the situation, that his day in court would come and then everybody would find the truth, that Stormy was innocent, that he hadn't laid a hand on that girl.

The truth.

The truth.

The truth.

As for me, I spent the rest of the evening researching different ways to commit suicide. From what I gathered, the most painless ways were pills, carbon monoxide, or drowning. The most painful: razor blade, jumping, fire.[84]

I'd been taught that it was a sin to commit suicide.

But I also knew that it was a sin to be alive.

---

[83] Once Stormy was convicted and he found out about his mother's confession and his sister's letter, he was angry and depressed. Lizzy and Jessica both tried visiting him in prison several times. Each time, he refused. "I don't understand," he said. "I'll never understand. How could they do something like that? I didn't hurt Chloe. I would never hurt a girl. Why would they think that?"

[84] According to the Centers for Disease Control and Prevention, 51% of suicides are by firearms, 25% by suffocation/hanging, and 17% by poisoning. Less than one half of one percent are by fire.

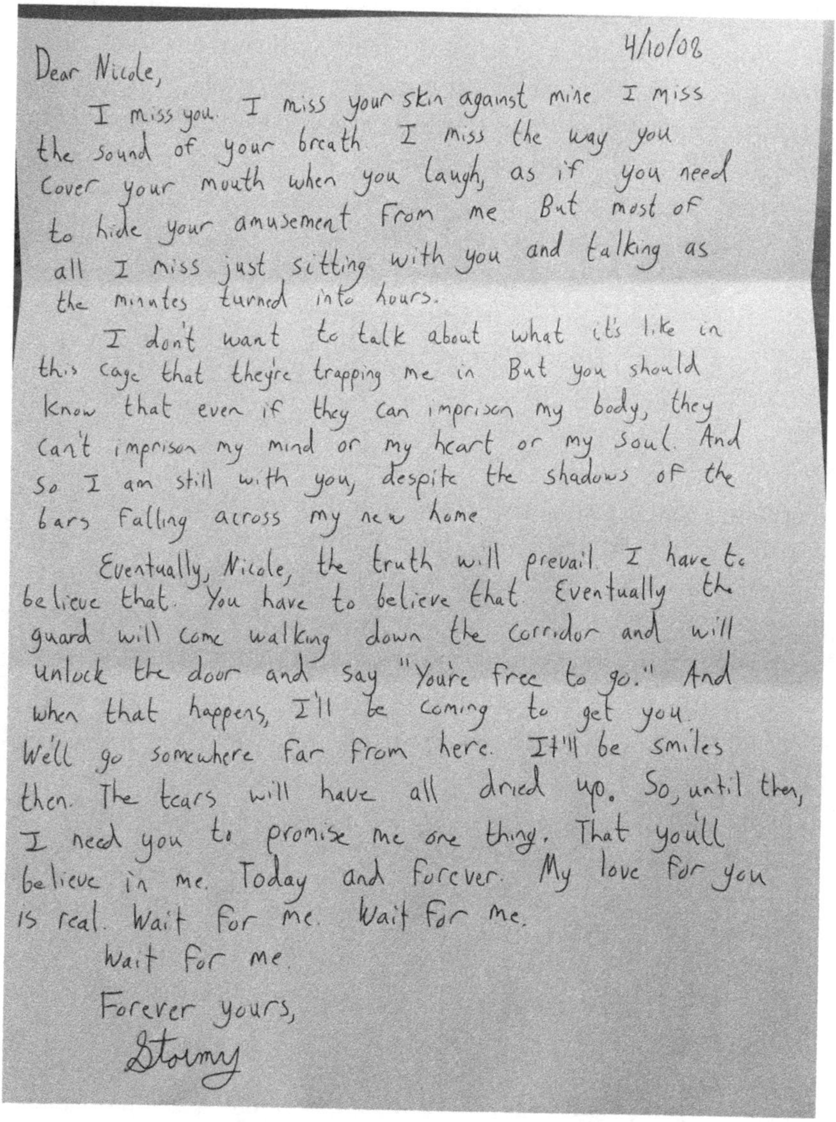

Dear Nicole,   4/10/08

        I miss you. I miss your skin against mine I miss
the sound of your breath. I miss the way you
cover your mouth when you laugh, as if you need
to hide your amusement from me But most of
all I miss just sitting with you and talking as
the minutes turned into hours.

        I don't want to talk about what it's like in
this cage that they're trapping me in But you should
know that even if they can imprison my body, they
can't imprison my mind or my heart or my soul. And
so I am still with you, despite the shadows of the
bars falling across my new home

        Eventually, Nicole, the truth will prevail. I have to
believe that. You have to believe that. Eventually the
guard will come walking down the corridor and will
unlock the door and say "You're free to go." And
when that happens, I'll be coming to get you.
We'll go somewhere far from here. It'll be smiles
then. The tears will have all dried up. So, until then,
I need you to promise me one thing. That you'll
believe in me. Today and forever. My love for you
is real. Wait for me. Wait for me.

        Wait for me.

        Forever yours,

        Stormy

Figure 17: One of many letters written from Stormy to Nicole, begging
her to wait for him while he was prison. She wrote back each and every
time, always promising that she would. During this time, Stormy did
not write to his mother. He did not write to his sister. Sadly, he never
spoke to his sister again.

CHAPTER 20

"But enough tall tales," said Dr. Pee Pee, "I think it is time that you tell us what really happened on the night that Chloe was killed."

"Fuck you."

"That's good, Lizzy. We're making some real break-throughs."[85]

---

[85] "I was not looking for a confession," Dr. Waugh said. "I only wanted her soul to be freed."

PART 3

CHAPTER 21

The night that Chloe died, I followed Stormy into the mountains. He never knew that I was behind him, never knew he was being watched (I have the power of invisibility, don't you know?). Yes, I'd stood in my bedroom window and watched as he raced across the front lawn.[86] I'd thrown on a black hoodie and a black hat and then tiptoed down the stairs and out the front door. Mother didn't hear me. She never knew I'd left. Once outside, I walked quickly, stepping over a passed-out drunk and avoiding a religious zealot, until I spotted him ahead, hands buried in his pockets. I stayed some ways behind, forever the shadow girl. Through town, into the hills, and toward Hagerman Tunnel, where the Lantern Man whistled that single murderous note.

As the sky turned to black and the wind moaned in agony, I hid behind the olden trees, watching my brother do the same. Between the gaps in my fingers, I watched as those boys, nothing but filthy monkeys, writhed and thrashed and grunted before

---

[86] While she didn't expand on it, her earlier narrative makes it clear that she watched Stormy leave the house. It is entirely conceivable, then, that Lizzy followed Stormy to Hagerman Tunnel. After all, she certainly had a history of tailing her brother. "She might have followed me," Stormy said. "She might have. I remember hearing footsteps. I remember seeing a figure behind me. I pushed it out of my consciousness, though. Do you think she followed me? That might explain some things." There is also no clear indication that she was home during the time of the murder. "I assumed she was in bed," Jessica Greiner said. "But I never checked. She could have been gone. She could have been at Hagerman Tunnel."

finally ejaculating into and onto Chloe. And then I watched as the boys dressed in the moonlight, laughing all the while, and left that poor girl to shiver all alone.

Stormy watched too, of course.

But an important question: why didn't Stormy go home, right then? A simple answer. Because fate wouldn't let him. Because fate grabs its victims by the ankles and drags them across the muddy floor and into the filthy water to bubble and bleed. "Hello," he said to Chloe, his voice calm. And I watched.

Remember when Jesus got on his high horse and said, "Everyone on the side of truth listens to me"? But old Pontius Pilate was ready and responded with the single greatest line in the Bible: "What is truth?" Because there is always more than one truth, depending on who's speaking, at what time, and under what circumstances.

My truth. He made love to her.[87]

But not the way those boys had done it. They had ravaged her, tearing her skin and pounding her body for one purpose and one purpose only: an animalistic self-gratification.

Stormy held her. Stormy loved her. He kissed her breasts and her thighs. He touched her cheek softly with his fingers. He whispered that he loved her, that he'd always loved her, that "thy eternal summer shall not fade, nor lose possession of that fair thou ow'st."

She moaned in bliss. She screamed in ecstasy.[88]

He never hit her. He never got violent with her. That's the truth.

When they were done making love, he held her in his arms

---

[87] Stormy denied having sex with Chloe and his DNA was not found on her body. Keep in mind, however, that her body had been submerged in water for several weeks, so the chances of any DNA recovery were slim. (The DNA of Billy and Josh—both of whom admitted to having sexual intercourse with Chloe—were also not recovered.)

[88] I have detailed Lizzy's pathological jealousy regarding her brother. If she had indeed witnessed Stormy engaged in sexual relations with Chloe, one can only imagine the type of rage she might have felt.

for an hour or two hours or more.

And the whole time, I watched.

"What about tomorrow?" Chloe asked. "What will you say when you see me in class?"

Stormy smiled and caressed her cheek. "I'll whisper something silly to make you laugh because I am not poetic enough to make you cry. But what you'll know is that my now-swollen heart will ache every single moment it is far from you. Until the day I die, leaves covering dirt covering my softening flesh."

"Oh, Stormy," Chloe said. "Why does this night have to end? Why can't God make an exception? Why does time have to march on to that insufferable beat?"

Why indeed?

Stormy offered to walk Chloe home because Stormy was a gentleman. The other boys had left her all alone in the cold and the dark, but not Stormy. "Come with me," he said. "Otherwise a bear or something worse is bound to get you."

Something worse.

But she only shook her head. "You go," she said. "I want to stay here for a bit. Some people are scared by the darkness. I'm comforted by it."

He touched her bare shoulder. "Are you sure?"

She nodded her head and smiled. "Yes. I'm sure. And then when I see you next, you'll whisper something silly to make me laugh. Because you're not poetic enough to make me cry."

"That's right," he said.

They kissed again and then he vanished into the darkness of the forest.

So it was just Chloe. All by herself.

But, no. That's wrong. I was there. Watching still. And listening, too. Listening to that whistle, that single note, getting louder and louder. The Lantern Man. With this hand he burns.

I could have saved her. That's what I believed and that's what I believe. But I was a coward and remained hidden in the darkness. I saw a flash of light and then I heard the screams,

Chloe's screams, echoing through the forest. I covered my eyes, but still I could see. The monster was upon her. He placed his hand over her mouth, muting her terror. He kissed her on the cheek and then snapped her head back. Death came quickly. He didn't mean for her to suffer. He remained with her for some time, a shroud of darkness over her body. And then he was gone, his black cape flowing in the wind. He left the shell behind, taking only her insides (heart, soul, humanity).

What is truth?

I seem to remember something else. Standing over Chloe. Her eyes were fluttering. "Who are you?" she said.

No, that's wrong. She was already dead. The Lantern Man had killed her.

What is truth?

Rage filled my throat, causing me to choke. I grabbed a rock that was nearby. With the devil guiding my arm, I came down hard, smattering her skull into eight identical pieces. Still she breathed and still she crawled.

"Die, you fucking bitch!"

But, no. It was the Lantern Man. Can't you feel him breathing on your neck?

"You can't have my brother! Not now! Not ever."

Not ever...

The blood is beneath my skin. And the only way to scrub myself clean is to first tear off that skin.

You're losing your mind, goddammit. It was the Lantern Man. Not you. He killed Chloe. He killed them all.

Every last one of them.

And so now. The fire. Yes. What the hell do I have to lose?[89]

---

[89] Unless we are to believe in ghosts, unless we are to believe in a boogeyman who carries a lantern and "searches for children who have strayed too far from the path to keep him eternal company in his cold, abandoned tunnel," it would seem that Lizzy Greiner has confessed to the act of murder. It would seem that Lizzy followed her brother into the woods and watched as he made love to Chloe Peterson. It would seem that she waited until he left. Then, in a fit of jealousy, it would seem that she smashed

Chloe's skull, killing her.

But, as you should well know by now, things aren't always what they seem.

It was on July 26th of this year that I received a phone call from a woman named Grace Patterson Miller. She was one of the girls who had been camping with Annie Gaddis back in 1973 when Annie had gone missing, never to be found. It was she who had reported seeing a tall man with shoulder-length blond hair carrying an old-fashioned mining lantern in the hours before Annie had gone missing. Previously, I had tried calling Mrs. Miller on several occasions without any luck. I thanked her for finally returning my call.

At first, she was reticent, but eventually she opened up.

She said, "You wouldn't think it would be painful after all of these years, but it is. I can still picture her smile. Still hear her laugh."

"I'm sorry," I said. "I know some pain never dulls completely."

"Yeah, well. I know that too well." A long pause and then, "Can I ask you a question? Why are you interested in Annie? I mean, she's been gone for an awful long time."

"It's a good question. To be honest with you, it's related to another case I'm investigating. Her disappearance bears some similarities. I've learned that you just never know where leads will take you."

For a few moments, she was quiet. Then she spoke again. "Okay, then. Something you should know. You're not the only one asking about Annie."

"What do you mean?"

"Another man came by my house. Just the other day. He asked if I had been with Annie the night she'd died. Then he showed me some pictures."

"Some pictures?"

"Yes. Of the Lantern Man."

I didn't think I'd heard her right.

"Did you say the Lantern Man?"

"Yes. I've got them in my hand if you'd like to see them."

Grace Miller lived in Sterling, on the eastern plains, about a three-and-half-hour drive from Leadville. Her house was a little bungalow in a working-class neighborhood, just a few blocks from the railroad tracks. When I arrived, she was sitting on her front porch, smoking a cigarette and drinking a Diet Coke. She rose to her feet but waited on her porch as I parked and walked across her neatly trimmed lawn. Grace was now in her early fifties, long graying hair tied in a bun.

"You must be Detective Buchanan," she said.

"Yes, ma'am."

"Come inside. Can I get you something to drink? Diet Coke? Lemonade?"

"A lemonade would be wonderful."

Her living room was cramped but neat, with a couple of couches angled toward a television, and bric-a-brac and family photographs lining the mantel. A burly man with a thick handlebar mustache appeared and introduced himself as Jim Miller, Grace's husband. He shook my hand and then disappeared down the hallway. I didn't see him again.

Grace returned from the kitchen with my lemonade. She sat down on one of the couches and I sat down on the other one. I pulled out my notebook, gathered my thoughts, and then spoke.

"Before we talk about the photographs, before we talk about the man who gave you the photographs, I'd like to ask you a few questions about what happened that weekend in 1973. Is that okay?"

"Yes. I remember some things clearly. Some things barely at all."

"Of course. And just so I understand. You were friends with Annie Gaddis, correct?"

She nodded her head. "Yes. We were like sisters."

"And the weekend in question. You went camping with her?"

"That's right. There were four of us. Me, Annie, Susan, and Meg."

"Are you still in touch with Susan or Meg?"

"Meg was the matron of honor at my wedding. I still see her from time to time. I haven't seen Susan since high school."

"And when you girls went camping. Your parents knew about it?"

"Sure. We'd done it a couple times before. It was a different time back then."

"Yes, it was. In the newspaper article, it said that Annie had been drinking heavily. Is that true?"

"Yes. Actually, we were all drinking. But she was drinking more than the rest of us."

"And you were quoted as saying that you left her behind to go look for wood. That she had talked about hurting herself."

"That's right."

"When she went missing, is that what you thought? That Annie had done something to herself?"

Grace grabbed a cigarette from a coffee table, stuck it in her mouth, and lit it. Her eyes turned to slits as she sucked down the smoke, then she nodded her head slowly. "Yup. That's what I thought at first. That maybe she had run away. Gone to a lake or something. Drowned herself."

"Do you think that now?"

She shook her head. "They never found her body, Detective. If she had taken her own life, they would have found her body, don't you think?"

"Most likely. Okay, then. Tell me about the man you saw before Annie went missing."

Grace tapped her cigarette on the ash tray and then her eyes rolled upward, fluttering open and closed in recollection. "We were setting up our tents," she said. "Just laughing and having fun. Drinking some beer. He appeared out of nowhere. He startled us. He was tall and thin. Long, blond hair. And the strangest thing: he carried a lantern. He looked like a ghost."

I jotted down some notes quickly in my pad and then flipped the page. "And this man. Did he say anything to you? Or did he just appear and leave?"

Grace's lips spread into a quivering grin. "Well. He stood there for a long time, just staring at us. It was creepy. Meg asked what he wanted. And still he didn't answer. Then he spoke, but his voice was really quiet."

"What did he say?"

"Like I said, he was very quiet. Barely louder than a whisper. But I think I heard. I think he said, 'I'm gonna eat you up.'"

The same threat he'd made about Donna Roswell. I dropped my pen to my pad and stared at Grace. "That's an odd thing to say."

"Yes. Of course, I might have misheard him. But I think that's what he said."

"Anything else?"

"No. He turned and walked away. Me and the girls laughed about him. It was creepy and we were all scared, but we just laughed. And then within an hour, we'd forgotten all about him."

"But after Annie went missing, you remembered him."

"Yes."

"And you told the cops?"

"Yes. They said they'd search for him. I don't think they ever found him, though. Time moves on. Her body was never recovered. The case went cold. Of course, in a small town, word gets around. Soon people were talking about him. About the Lantern Man. 'Don't go into the woods,' parents would say. 'The Lantern Man will get you.'"

"I don't think parents ever stopped telling that story," I said.

"No. I suppose not."

I sighed deeply and took a drink of my lemonade. I was trying not to get ahead of myself, but these connections seemed to be more than coincidences. Missing girls. A man with a lantern. Threatening to eat them. "Okay," I said. "Let's move to the present. You said that a man recently showed up at your house."

"That's right."

"What day was that?"

She looked up at the ceiling, thinking. "Well, jeez. I guess it was Monday morning. I was sitting in the kitchen reading a magazine when he knocked."

"Did he tell you his name?"

"No, sir, he didn't."

"And what did he look like?"

"He wasn't dressed like a detective, that's for sure. He wore overalls and a baseball hat. His face was unshaven. He looked homeless, to be honest with you."

I cleared my throat. "And what did he say?"

"He asked me if I was Grace Patterson. I said that was my maiden name. And then I asked how I could help him. He looked like he was about to cry. He asked me if I was friends with Annie Gaddis. The question caught me by surprise. I didn't answer, but I guess my expression must have revealed the truth. He said, 'I'm sorry showing up to your house unannounced. But I'm trying to figure out who killed Annie.' I didn't know what to say. So I didn't say anything. He asked if he could come in. I told him that wasn't a good idea. Then he reached into his overall pocket and pulled out an envelope. Inside were several photographs. He handed them to me. He asked me if I recognized the man. Asked if he was the Lantern Man I'd seen so many years ago."

Grace stopped speaking. She crushed out her cigarette and quickly reached for another. "And so?" I said. "Did you recognize him?"

She breathed deeply and closed her eyes. "It had been so many years."

"Thirty-five."

"But I recognized him. There wasn't a doubt in my mind."

"And did you tell him that?"

She shook her head. "No. For some reason, I told him that I didn't recognize him. I don't know why."

"And did he ask any other questions?"

"No. But he left the photographs with me. He said, 'Keep them. Maybe you'll remember him one day.' Then he left."

"And you haven't heard back from him?"

"No."

I tapped my pen on my pad. "Can I see the photographs?"

"Yes, sir." She grabbed a romance novel from the coffee table, flipped through some pages, and pulled out the photos. Then she reached over and handed them to me.

There were three photographs. In each photograph was the same un-smiling man. In one of the photos, he was young with long blond hair. In another, he was middle-aged, his hair still long, but graying. And in the last photograph, the only one in color, he looked old and feeble. But it was the same man. That was certain.

"And which version of the Lantern Man did you recognize?" I asked.

"The young version. The one with blond hair."

I studied the photos for a few minutes. "Mind if I hold on to these?"

She shook her head. "I don't want them. They'll give me nightmares."

We spoke for a while more. She told me all about Annie. I think it was cathartic for her.

Eventually, I rose to my feet. "Thank you very much, Mrs. Miller. This has all been very helpful."

"So what do you think? Do you think that man in the photos is the one who killed my friend?"

I shook my head. "I don't know. Maybe. These things are hard to say for certain."

I packed up my things and began walking toward the door. I had just taken a step outside, when Mrs. Miller called my name. I turned around.

"There's just one more thing," she said.

"What's that?"

"I got the stranger's license plate number. If that helps you."

I learned that the stranger's name was Oliver Fischer. He worked as the manager of the Dollar Store and was unmarried. He had no criminal record. The next day I went to his store to pay him a visit. A teenage sales clerk directed me to an office in the back of the store. I rapped on the door a few times and waited. A gruff voice said, "What do you want?"

"Mr. Fischer? My name is Russ Buchanan. I'm with the Leadville Police. I have a few questions for you."

No response. I knocked again.

"Hold on," he said, then, a few moments later, the door creaked opened. He was a heavy-set man, his eyes just narrow slits in a doughy face.

"Detective Buchanan," I said again and showed him my badge. "Do you have a few minutes?"

"What's this about?"

I pulled out the photographs. "Why don't you tell me?"

He glanced quickly at the photographs and then looked away. "I got nothing to say."

"Mr. Fischer, why did you show up unannounced at Grace Miller's house? Why'd you give her these pictures?"

His face reddened and his jaw clenched. "I got nothing to say," he said again. Then he pushed the door closed.

I pulled out a contact card and shoved it beneath the door. Then I left.

A week later, Fischer called. I knew he would. It was late in the evening, nearly midnight. "It's Oliver Fischer," he said. "I've got some things to tell you."

"I'm listening."

"But not over the phone. How about the Ice Palace Park? In thirty minutes."

"Sure. I'll see you there."

He hung up the phone.

Outside the air was still mild, and the sky was black and filled with a thousand dead stars. I arrived at the park, sat down on a bench, folded my arms behind my head, and waited. At a few minutes past ten o'clock, I heard a voice.

"Detective Buchanan?"

I turned around.

Fischer stood a few yards back, his figure revealed by the moonlight and a distant street lamp.

"Yes. Hi, Mr. Fischer."

He glanced around furtively before walking around the bench and sitting down next to me. He folded his hands in his lap, as if he was waiting for the bus. I could hear him wheezing, but he didn't speak, not for a long time.

Finally: "I know some things about the Lantern Man," he said. He was breathing loudly. "I know a lot of things."

He reached into his pocket. At first, I thought he was reaching for a package of cigarettes, but instead it was an inhaler. He placed it to his mouth and sucked down the medicine. His breathing became softer and he began nodding his head for such a long time that I wondered if he'd ever stop.

"Okay," I said. "What, exactly, do you know?"

"Well, let's start with this," he said. "The Lantern Man is my father."

I didn't respond right away, surprised by his statement.

"Is that right?"

"Yes. That is, I think so. One can never be sure. About anything."

"No. I guess you can't. And that's why you visited Mrs. Miller? To see if she remembered him? I'll bet you were hoping she couldn't."

He sighed deeply and squeezed his eyes shut. A few more minutes passed before Fischer spoke again. Now his voice seemed gentler somehow. "What you should know about my dad is that he was a good father. He taught me how to play baseball, how to throw a curve ball. When I was eight years old, he bought me a train set and helped me put it together. He never raised his voice in anger. He never placed a hand on me."

"Yes," I said. "He does sound like a good man."

"My mother died three years ago. Breast cancer. It was too bad. By that point, he really depended on her. After she passed, the old man wasn't the same. Just a shell of his former self. To help out, I began coming to the old man's house every Saturday. At first it wasn't so bad. He enjoyed the company. But it wasn't long until his body started going. And his mind, too. Eventually it got so bad that he could barely take care of himself. He would just sit in his recliner chair staring straight ahead, whistling a single note. I told him that maybe we should find him a home, but he refused. 'I'll die in my house,' he said. 'That's the way I want it.'"

Whistling a single note. Fischer stopped speaking for a moment and again pulled out his inhaler. Another two puffs and he cleared his throat and rubbed his hands together.

"It was early March of this year when Dad's heater started malfunctioning. I asked him if he wanted me to work on fixing it, but he said he'd already called a guy. Said he was going to come first thing on Monday. I should have never listened to him. It was a cold week that week. You know how it gets in Leadville. The heater was never fixed. He'd probably never called. When I came to visit him the next week, I found him in bed, covered with blankets. His face was pale blue and his eyes were open. The poor bastard had frozen himself to death."

Just like Baby Doe, I thought.

"I'm sorry," I said, "for your loss."

"Yeah, well. It happens to all of us. Sooner it later. So anyway, they came and took the body. Funeral arrangements were arranged. I waited until he was decently in the ground before I got to work on cleaning out the house. He and Mom had been accumulating junk since the time I was a kid. I don't think they'd gotten rid of a thing. Bowling trophies and broken radios and dresses and suits. You get the idea. It took me weeks to sift through everything. My sister lives in Davenport, Iowa, and she told me that the only thing she wanted was Mom and Dad's old record collection. Mom loved Frank Sinatra and Dad loved Little Richard and Bill Haley and so they owned quite a few of their records. My sister coveted those. The rest she told me I could keep or toss. But I've never been particularly nostalgic, so I took to trashing almost everything, although I did keep a handful of photos and a few books. Anyway, I had just about finished cleaning the house when I recalled that there was still one room that I hadn't cleaned, one room that I hadn't seen, in fact, since I was a young child."

Fischer fell silent. For a while, I thought I could hear him sobbing, but I soon realized that it was just the wind.

"A room that you hadn't seen? In your own childhood home?"

He nodded and said, "In the back hallway, there's a stairway that leads to the attic floor. When we were very little, my sister and I used to spend a lot of time up there, just playing and exploring. Back then, there wasn't much up there except a bunch of boxes and old paintings and sewing machines. At least that's what I remember. And then, at some point, my mother told us that we could no longer go up into that attic."

"Did she say why?"

"She did. She said that it was dangerous for us. She said that the Lantern Man was known to hide in the attics of children's houses, and if they went up there he was bound to capture them in his magical burlap sack. It was just a story, but it got us scared enough."

"I've heard a similar story before."

"Flash forward to his death. I knew I needed to go up there, but even after all of these years, I was pretty anxious. I think, as a child, I had convinced myself that the Lantern Man actually spent his nights in that top floor. And the fear never really left. It sounds silly, but I really had to muster up a lot of courage to go in."

"Not silly at all."

"Anyway," he said, in a voice barely louder than a whisper. "I did muster up the courage, eventually. I climbed those stairs. I unlocked the door. I pushed it open. And then I stepped inside."

"And...what did you see?"

No answer.

"What did you see?" I asked again.

"It's hard to know exactly."

"What do you mean?"

And now he turned to me, and I could see that his eyes were glazed with fear. "Maybe, Detective, you should see for yourself."

It wasn't for another five days that I finally did.

His father, the one Oliver claimed to be the Lantern Man, was named Horst Fischer. Mr. Fischer was born on September 25th, 1948, to Hans and Ellen Fischer (both deceased) in Winterset, Iowa, and moved to Longmont, Colorado, in 1968. There he worked at the turkey plant for a few years, but he quit that job in 1972 and moved to Leadville with his new wife, Mary. (She spent twenty-eight years as a beloved first-grade teacher at Westpark Elementary School over on W. 12th St.) Horst Fischer, meanwhile, bounced from job to job, never staying at one place for more than two years. Some of his jobs included working as a mailman, a gas station attendant, a short-order cook, and a custodian. He didn't seem to have many friends, and I was only able to talk to a couple of people who remembered him at all. One was named Joey Hoffman, who worked at the post office. He described Fischer as a tall and gawky fellow, one who didn't say much but seemed to get all of his work done. According to Hoffman, he was friendly enough, but he did have an odd way of walking, as if he were stepping over puddle after puddle. Another man, Buddy Hines, said that he had drinks with him a few times after work (gas station), but he didn't find out much about him other than he despised Richard Nixon.

Fischer had no criminal record—I couldn't even find any speeding or parking tickets. The only mention I could find of him in any public records was for the purchase of his house for $18,000 in 1975. But there was one mention of him in the newspaper, from 1978. Apparently, he volunteered at the First Presbyterian, working with youth.

Due to HIPAA, I was unable to access any of his medical records. However, Dr. Earl MacGregor (whom I consider a friend) remembered treating him in the late 1980s for a case of recurring gout. His most vivid memory is not of the gout itself, but instead some odd questions that Horst Fischer asked him about the ailment. He asked the doctor if it was possible that his diet was causing the gout. He mentioned that he'd recently visited China and had eaten some exotic delicacies including monkey brain and stewed dog. In particular, he was quite concerned about the effect of eating the brain. Dr. MacGregor assured him that there was likely no relation and that seemed to placate Fischer. However, since serving monkey brain in China has been illegal for many decades, I find it unlikely that he actually ate this bizarre dinner. A disturbing thought to consider: perhaps Fischer was instead referring to another type of "delicacy." Was he referring to eating human flesh? Remember the strange letter that Mr. Roswell received? "i decid id eat her just like fish so i did but he was rong she didnt tast good more like undercooked chiken but mabe i didnt coke her long enugh..." Remember him threatening to eat those girls?

On August 10, 2008, I drove out to County Road 11½ to the house where Horst Fischer had died (see note 34 for an earlier mention of the house). It was a big farmhouse that had once been white but now was rotting and collapsing toward the dirt. With the majestic peaks of Mount Massive coloring the background, it was the only house visible for miles.

Oliver was waiting for me when I arrived. He was sitting on the front steps, a cigarette in one hand and an inhaler in the other. I parked my truck in the driveway and stepped outside. The wind was blowing, and I shielded my eyes from the dirt and dust that was whipping around the property.

I reached out my hand to shake his, but he didn't reciprocate. Instead, he just said, "Follow me."

He unlocked the wooden door—splintered down the middle—and pushed it open. The blinds were all closed and so it was dim despite the time of day. Nothing remained in the house—not even any furniture—but still it smelled of illness and death. When Oliver turned on a light, I could see the dust spinning slowly toward the ceiling.

Floorboards creaking beneath our feet, I followed him through the empty living room and kitchen and down a narrow hallway where a single painting of a tree remained forgotten on the peeling wall. We reached the end of the hallway and came to a staircase that led to the region above the ceiling. Up here was the room that Oliver and his sister had been forbidden to enter since they were children. Because that's where the Lantern Man waited.

"It's unlocked," he said grimly.

I assumed he would be entering the attic with me, but as soon as I started climbing the stairs, he gave me a quick glance and, without a word, walked back down the hallway and out the front door.

The door was wooden and had to be pulled down from the ceiling with a thin nylon rope. It took several tugs before it finally creaked open. I placed both of my arms above the frame and pulled myself upward, struggling to get my feet onto solid ground. Once upright I reached into my pocket and pulled out a small flashlight. I moved the light back and forth, up and down. I saw boxes and crates and chests. Piles of clothes and empty easels. And then something else. Lanterns. Dozens of them, all of them old-fashioned like the ones miners used to use. I felt my heartbeat quickening and my breath shallowing. *His ghost wanders through the forest each and every night, his lantern bouncing up and down, creating menacing shadows.* Cautiously, I took a few steps forward and placed my hand on a large, black chest-of-drawers. It was unlocked, so I pulled it open. The chest was stuffed-full with dresses and shoes and little jackets. The clothes of children. *He can smell the sweet flesh of children, and so once he finds them he follows them silently, staying hidden behind the boughs of the forest.*

And now, my flashlight swung to the left. On the far wall was a single cross and a painting of a bleach-blond Jesus. Beneath the painting was a large piece of corkboard, and on the corkboard were photographs. I took a few steps forward. Girls, so many girls. Some of them were as young as ten or eleven years old; some appeared to be teenagers. Many of the photos were in black-and-white and, judging from the clothes and hairstyles, appeared to have been taken a long time ago. Some looked to be from more recent times. They looked terrified, these girls, as if they knew their fate but were helpless to prevent it. Had Fischer, the Lantern Man, taken these photos before killing them? My hands were trembling, but I kept looking. I knew who these girls were. I knew. Annie Gaddis. Donna Roswell. Who else? Who else? I moved my flashlight up and down, back and forth, dread covering my skin. I took a step away and then another. He'd killed them all. The Lantern Man. And I was about to scurry back down the staircase, when I noticed something else. On the bottom corner of the corkboard there was a photograph that had been torn away. All that remained were her eyes, gazing with terror. For several minutes, I frantically searched the floor trying to locate the rest of the photograph. It was no use. But I didn't really need the rest of her face to identify her. I knew whose eyes I was looking at.

Chloe Peterson.

Figure 18: From top to bottom: One of the many lanterns located in Fischer's attic; Horst Fischer, months before his death; the house where Fischer lived.

CHAPTER 22

About a half mile from Hagerman Tunnel there was an old ghost town called Douglass City.[90] I couldn't help but wonder if the Lantern Man lived here, back when he was a man instead of a monster. I wondered if he had loved a woman. I wonder if that woman had loved him. All of the structures had rotted and turned to rubble. All except one. I'd heard that it was called the Smith House, as if giving it a name could provide it with dignity. It was really nothing more than a shack and didn't seem to have long for this world. The wood was decaying and the metal roof was collapsing. But there was still a working door and enough shelter to keep you protected from the wind and the snow. I figured that, eventually, they would come searching for me, just like they searched for Shannon, just like they searched for Chloe. But for the time being, I was all alone. For the time being, I sat and waited. For his death. For my death.

I stole enough food and juice from my house to last a few days if necessary. But I didn't think I would be here for very long. I had a warm blanket. I had my journal. And I had fire. Because that's how I would destroy the Lantern Man when the time was at hand.

---

[90] Lizzy did not show up for the last two days of school. The attendance secretary left a message with Jessica, but she did not check her phone. Despite the fact that her daughter was also missing from home, Jessica did not call the authorities.

During the day, I slept and ate and thought. My sleep was mainly full of nightmares, and my thoughts were maybe worse. Mostly I thought about Chloe, in that darkened tunnel, and how she'd moaned in agony and bled in solitude. Sometimes I thought about Stormy and what he was doing in jail. He didn't belong there, and I doubted he'd survive. I'd heard stories, of course, about cruelty and degradation. It was a bunch rotten circumstances that put him there, but I couldn't help but feel some of the burden. After all, I never should have written the letter. It was unfair of me. The truth: I was mad and hurt and wanted him to pay. But Stormy didn't kill Chloe. It was the Lantern Man. They wouldn't believe me, though, if I told them. They'd call me crazy, or something worse.

During the night, I wandered through the darkened woods, gripping my flashlight with one hand and pulling back branches with the others. I knew he was out here somewhere, waving his lantern and whistling that single note. But I couldn't go too far from the shack. Otherwise, he'd capture me and take me to Hagerman Tunnel. It had been several weeks since he'd eaten. Certainly, he was hungry for a soul.[91]

A few times, late at night, when the moon had vanished behind clouds, I thought I heard him whistling, thought I saw his mining lantern. But, no. The whistling was only the wind howling or an owl screeching, and the light was only the sky flashing or my head splitting.

I stayed up all night, not daring to squeeze my eyes shut for even a minute. I knew he could smell me. Knew he could see me. But, still, he stayed away. Did he sense the fuel and flame? Mourn his own mortality? Is that why he stayed away? But temptation is strong, even for the dead among us, and I knew he'd appear eventually.

As I mentioned, during the day, when I slept, I had horrifying nightmares. One such nightmare: I'm home, staring out the

---

[91] How many girls had Fischer killed? What had he done with them? Eaten them like he claimed in his letter?

window. Dead leaves fall from gnarled trees. A woman in black arrives with a storm, the darkened sky glowing white with each angry bolt of lightning, the asphalt and sidewalks blurring in the filthy rain. I remember her from my childhood: over her shoulder she balances a half-dozen scarecrows, hay spilling from flannel shirts, eyes and noses and mouths missing from burlap faces. The strange woman gazes at me and says, "I want you to listen to me, darling. The doctors. The therapists. Your family. They're wrong. They're wrong about everything. And you. You were right. You were always right." And then she strokes my cheek and says, "Goodbye, my beautiful angel. It's a shame the world has to be this way."

"Wait!" I call out. "Don't say goodbye. Please. Stay a little longer. I'm scared. I don't want to be all alone."

The old woman turns back toward me, black hood covering her eyes and says, "It's only flesh, my darling. And flesh is meant for the fire. I only wish I could help."

And then the old woman is gone, vanished into the dark, leaving nothing but scarecrows burned to embers.

Another nightmare: I'm with my father, and we're driving in the mountains, the pine trees guarding lost souls and the abandoned mines hiding horrific secrets. I'm uncertain what my father plans to do, but I know it will be horrific.

Deeper and deeper into the mountains, where a girl's screams would be muted by the wind and the hills and the trees. And now I'm outside the car, leaning against a tree, and my father walks toward me. Carrying a rope. Carrying a spike. And like Isaac in biblical times, I watch him curiously. That's when my father, with resignation in his eyes, places the spike on top of my foot and uses his carpenter's hammer to drive it through my flesh. My screams echo through the mountains and I writhe on the ground. My father bends down, picks me up, and carries me across the forest floor, and all the while I'm sobbing and praying. He ties me to a tree and I plead with him, but he backs away weeping and gnashing his teeth. And as he gets into his car and drives away, I see a murder of crows circling the tree.

And now I see my father from above, and he drives until he comes to a lake that's absolutely still. He drinks some vodka and then some more. He steps out of the car and fills his pockets with a thousand tiny stones. Then he walks slowly into the lake. The water gets deeper and deeper, and soon it is just his eyes peeking above the water and then he is no more.

Yes, these were dreams, I was sure, but I have to admit that sometimes it was hard to tell the difference between wakefulness and slumber, between lucidity and lunacy. My senses were coming apart at the seams.

So on that black night when I first heard the muted whistling, I was uncertain if I was dreaming. I was standing near a river, puffs of steam pluming from my mouth. My hands were numb despite being buried in my pockets. When I first heard that familiar sound, my ears pricked and I stopped in my tracks. I fell to my knees and held my breath. I waited there for a long time, but all was silence. Eventually, I got enough courage to rise to my feet and move forward. But I hadn't gone more than twenty feet when I heard the whistling again. This time, it was louder and more distinct. It was him, I was sure of it.

I moved quickly through the woods, my heart pounding hard. And, like the first time I encountered the Lantern Man, I moved toward the sound, not away from it. Long minutes passed, and the whistling remained, but I never seemed to get closer. How dark was the sky, dead stars hidden behind clouds. I began talking out loud. "I know you're there," I said. "You don't scare me. You killed those girls, and now I aim to kill you."

More whistling and now it was getting louder.

"And your soul will be swallowed into the abyss."

I heard the rustling of leaves. The whistling stopped. Had he vanished into the night? I held my breath and remained where I was. I waited for a minute, two minutes, three. He was gone. I exhaled deeply and took a step forward.

And that's when I saw him.

He was maybe a dozen feet away. I might have let out a scream, and he swung his head toward me. For a moment, I was paralyzed, and now the Lantern Man moved toward me, his eyes empty yet staring right at me.[92]

Somebody whispered in my ear, "Go, Lizzy! Go." And so I did.

I darted onto an olden path, the blackened pine trees swaying menacingly above. I ran as fast as I could, my heart rattling in my rib cage. I didn't dare look back, but I knew the Lantern Man was behind me, waiting to add my soul to his never-ending collection.

And now suddenly it was snowing (or had it been snowing this whole time?), and the snow was blowing directly into my face, making it almost impossible to see. I could hear my own breath, hear my feet crunching on the snow beneath. I kept waiting to feel the Lantern Man's cold hands pressing against the skin of my neck, but it didn't happen.

How long did I run? A few minutes? An hour? A day? Time had lost all meaning for me. Eventually I saw the decrepit shack (A Swelling of the Ground—The Roof was scarcely visible—The Cornice—in the Ground—) and I pushed through the door and pulled it shut behind me. My hands were trembling badly, from the cold and from my fear, and I couldn't get them to behave. It took me a long time to empty the two cans of kerosene, but soon the floor was soaked, just like that of Hinnom.[93] I removed my Bic lighter from my pocket and slid down against the wall. My cheeks were slathered with tears and my heart was aching with fear. But still I remained. And still I waited.

I waited for hours. I waited for days. Sometimes I breathed. Sometimes I didn't. I wondered about Shannon and what her final thoughts were. Did she think about Stormy? Did she think

---

[92] Did she see really see him all these times? Did she see the Lantern Man? Did she see Horst Fischer? I still don't know for certain.

[93] From Jer. 7:31: "And they have built the high places of Tophet, which is in the valley of the son of Hinnom, to burn their sons and their daughters in the fire; which I commanded them not, neither came it into my heart."

about me? Were they thoughts of forgiveness? Or were they thoughts of hate?

I wondered about Chloe, too. She'd never had a chance. Not in this piss pot of a world. And what I thought, what I knew, is that it was the Lantern Man who killed her. Not me. Not me. Not me...[94]

He was outside, I was sure of it. I could hear the faint whistling, could see the flash of his lantern, and it wasn't just my delusions. Yes, he was outside. Waiting. Time meant nothing to him. But eventually he'd enter. He'd walk toward me slowly, the wood creaking beneath his feet. He'd speak, and it would be just two words: "It's time."[95]

But, for once in my life, I wouldn't be afraid.[96]

---

[94] Yes, Fischer. Not Lizzy. Not Stormy. That's what I believe.

[95] He searches for children who have strayed too far from the path to keep him eternal company in his cold, abandoned tunnel. Sometimes he strangles her. Sometimes he suffocates her. Sometimes he drowns her. Sometimes he burns her. But always he kills her.

[96] Always he kills her.

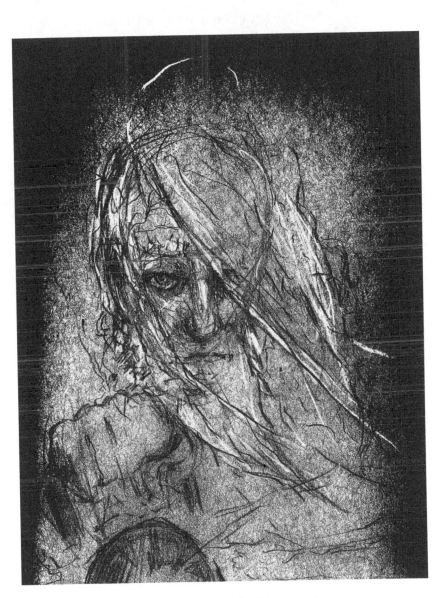

Figure 19: "It was the Lantern Man" by Lizzy Greiner.

Because I could not stop for Death
by Emily Dickinson (1830-1886)

Because I could not stop for Death—
He kindly stopped for me—
The Carriage held but just Ourselves—
And Immortality

We slowly drove—He knew no haste
And I had put away
My labor and my leisure too,
For His Civility—

We passed the School, where Children strove
At Recess—in the Ring—
We passed the Fields of Gazing Grain—
We passed the Setting Sun—

Or rather—He passed us—
The Dews drew quivering and chill—
For only Gossamer, my Gown—
My Tippet—only Tulle—

We paused before a House that seemed
A Swelling of the Ground—
The Roof was scarcely visible—
The Cornice—in the Ground—

Since then—'tis Centuries—and yet
Feels shorter than the Day
I first surmised the Horses' Heads
Were toward Eternity—

Leadville Toi

$1.00

October 14, 2008

Missing Girls' Bodies Found

by Michael Hampton

LEADVILLE — The remains of at least three bodies were discovered in a field on the outskirts of Leadville on Saturday morning.

One of the bodies was positively identified as Donna Roswell, who has been missing for more than twenty years. The other bodies have not yet been identified, but one of them is believed to be Annie Gaddis, who died in 1973.

The bodies were located on the property of Horst Fischer, a longtime Leadville resident who died earlier this year. It is believed that Fischer killed each of the girls before burying them.

For years, there have been rumblings about the so-called Lantern Man, a shadowy figure who haunts the mountains near Leadville. For the most part, the stories have been dismissed as nothing more than a local myth, but recently Leadville detective Russ Buchanan began suspecting his existence as he investigated the recent murder of Chloe Peterson, Fischer's son, Oliver, informed Buchanan that he suspected his father was the Lantern Man, and the detective eventually discovered several pieces of evidence at Horst Fischer's house. That lead to a department wide investigation into Fischer's past and eventually lead to the grisly discovery.

"I don't believe in ghosts," Detective Buchanan said. "But I certainly believe in human beings who act like monsters."

The recovery of Roswell's body brings to a close a high profile case that engulfed Leadville in 1986. While the murderer was never convicted and sentenced, Donna's father, Dan, is thankful that he can finally properly mourn the loss of his daughter.

"She was taken from me. She was taken from all of us. It's been twenty two years, but it doesn't seem longer than a month. I'll miss her every day, for as long as I live. But tonight I can sleep knowing that she's finally been found."

The police officer who eventually found the first body explained that within five minutes the second body had been found nearby. "It was pretty hard to believe. And then it wasn't Continued on page 2

Leadville Toi

$1.00   January 13, 2009

Conviction Overturned

by Michael Hampton

LEADVILLE — A judge on Wednesday overturned the conviction of Brandon "Stormy" Greiner, citing new evidence that casts doubt on the verdict.

Greiner, now eighteen years old, was recently sentenced to twenty years in prison for the murder of classmate Chloe Peterson. Her body was found in an undisclosed location in the ghost town of Gilman, having been moved there by Greiner's mother, Jessica. Jessica Greiner admitted to moving the body from the Hagerman Tunnel after she believed her son had killed Chloe.

However, local authorities recently have become convinced that it was not Stormy Greiner, but rather the so-called Lantern Man, Horst Fischer, who murdered Lizzy. Several bodies were discovered buried on his property. Meanwhile, a journal belonging to Stormy's sister, Lizzy, seemed to indicate Fischer's role in the murder. Of course, Fischer cannot be charged with the crime, since he died this past spring.

Chloe's mother, Lindsey Peterson, said that she's glad there's finally closure. "I had such mixed feelings when the Greiner boy was convicted," she said. "When I looked into his eyes, I didn't think he was capable of committing that

Brandon "Stormy" Greiner

crime. But Horst Fischer. He was capable. And there's a special place in hell for him."

The last year has been full of tragedy for the Greiner family. Last year, Shannon Greiner drowned when she was swimming with her two siblings at Opal Lake. Not long after that, Stormy Greiner was charged and convicted in the death of Chloe Peterson. And then this past spring, Lizzy perished, the result of a cabin fire

in the woods outside of Leadville. There have been some rumblings that her death was also caused by Fischer, although the Police Department has not commented on that matter.

"I have reached out to Jessica," Peterson said. "We've both experience so much pain. I hope that someday we can meet in person."

The detective credited with discovering the

Continued on page 2

LEADVILLE POLICE DEPARTMENT
800 Harrison Avenue, Leadville, CO 80461
(719) 486-1365

Chief Sam Mickel
March 11, 2009

Dear Detective Buchanan:

Once again, our deepest gratitude must be expressed for your outstanding investigative work on the Chloe Peterson case. The discovery that we had a monster living in our midst for so many years is shocking, but at least there can be some relief knowing that Horst Fischer was finally "outed," even if it came too late for the many girls who suffered at his hands, and even if it came too late for justice to be levied.

Jessica Greiner is, of course, forever thankful that her son, Stormy, has been exonerated and released from prison. I must admit that I am somewhat conflicted about his release. The truth is that we still don't know exactly what happened that night at Hagerman Tunnel. While Horst Fischer was most certainly a monster, did he kill Chloe Peterson? I have my doubts. With his other victims, Fischer disposed of the bodies. Why would he leave Peterson's body in the tunnel? Additionally, he had already fallen ill by that time, and I find it unlikely that he would have had the strength necessary to cause such a fatal trauma.

I find it more compelling that Lizzy Greiner was the murderer. After all, she certainly had motive—her journal makes it abundantly clear that she suffered from pathological jealousy regarding her brother. It has not been disproven that she followed her brother the night in question. It has not been disproven that she watched him make love to her. It has not been disproven that she waited until he left and then attacked Chloe Peterson.

And while this uncertainty will gnaw at me, I will do my best to keep it private. After all, our community needs to heal from these wounds. Adding doubt and ambiguity would only tear at the scabs. Therefore, it will remain in the public record our belief that Horst Fischer, the Lantern Man, killed Chloe Peterson by rock. He then killed Lizzy Greiner by fire.

Because we all need a narrative to get us through the day.

Sincerely,

Sam Mickel

Chief Sam Mickel

CHAPTER 23

Stormy Greiner
Ten Years Later

When I was just a kid—maybe eight-years old—I witnessed my first miracle. It was early summer in Leadville, nighttime, and the carnival was in town. Harrison Avenue, the main strip, was closed off to make room for all of the rides, like the Tilt-A-Whirl and Carousal and Kamikaze and Ferris Wheel. Me, I must have gone on that Kamikaze ten times or more, swinging backwards and forwards, backward and forwards, terrified, screaming my little head off. Other things I remember from that night: a girl in sequin twirling a baton; a man in a tuxedo walking on stilts. A fire juggler and a sword swallower and a mind reader. And then there was the magician. Yes, I remember him well.

He stood in front of the old Tabor Opera House, a three-story building made of stone and brick and Portland cement. On the wrought iron fence, the magician hung a banner, "The Amazing Resurrector," colored in bright orange, yellow, and red.

The magician was an obese man, and sweat slathered his face. He wore black pants, a white dress shirt with the sleeves rolled up, a black vest, and a black necktie. A porkpie hat lay askew on his head. There wasn't much of a crowd because people didn't think he was much of a magician. They were wrong. While the streetlamps flickered above, he made a coin vanish and stole somebody's watch and guessed somebody's playing card. A few people applauded. Most people left. I was transfixed.

At some point, with much pomp and circumstance, he lifted a piece of cloth, revealing a caged rabbit. By this time, other than a drunk or two, I might have been the only person watching. The magician took an interest in me, winking and grinning, giving me the business. "And then there was one," he said. "But, if you don't mind my saying so, you look like a magician yourself. In fact, I would venture to say that you possess some powers that you didn't even know you had."

I was shy, so I nodded without saying a word.

"And are you curious about your powers?"

"Yes," I said after a moment.

He showed me the rabbit up close. "Do you like him?" he asked. "Do you think he's precious? I've named him Whiskers. Can you figure out why?"

I thought this one over. "Because he has long whiskers, I think."

"That's right. *Exactly* right. I could tell you were a smart boy. And, now. Would you like to pet him?"

I nodded my head, yes. He moved the little bunny, nose twitching, toward me, and I smoothed its fur with my fingers. This rabbit was the cutest, most special thing in the entire world. I loved him. I wanted to take him home with me. But the love was short lived because at that moment the magician snatched Whiskers away from me. Teeth bared and eyes wild, he raised the animal high in the air and then proceeded to slam him against the pavement, once, twice, three times. I was too shocked to scream; instead, I just stared at little Whiskers, now a pile of blood and skin and bones, with my mouth open wide. And now the magician looked at me, and he grinned a sinister grin. "Oh, no," he said. "Little Whiskers has had an accident, a terrible accident. It looks like he's dead, doesn't it?"

I broke into tears, not so much because he'd killed the rabbit, but because for just a moment I had thought he was going to give me Whiskers to take home as a pet. I would have loved to have snuggled with him and petted him and fed him. He bent down until his fat red face was just inches from mine and said, "Oh, Lord. I hate that someone as smart as you is crying. Are you crying because of Whiskers' accident? Are you crying because Whiskers is dead? Is that why you're crying?"

I might have nodded my head.

"Wipe your eyes, little hero. Wipe your eyes." And now, with great care, he covered the mutilated rabbit with his hat. He looked up at me and grinned and winked. "Ah, come on. Wipe those tears from your eyes. It's not so bad. Do you know why they call me The Amazing Resurrector?"

I shook my head no.

"Well. A resurrection means to bring back to life. And so that's what I do. First, I kill. But then I bring back. Would you like me to bring back Whiskers?"

"Yes," I said. "Bring him back."

"I'd like very much to. Today, however, I'm a bit weak. Today, I think, I need your help. Do you remember how I told you that you have powers?"

"Yes," I whispered. "I remember."

"Well. You're going to use those powers to help me. To help Whiskers. Do you believe me?"

"I don't know."

He placed his wand into my hand. "I need you to believe. It's very important. And now, what I'd like you to do is to tap on the hat three times with this magic wand? Okay?"

I managed to stop crying, but my lower lip was still trembling. "Okay."

I was about to tap, but he grabbed my hand. "Oh. I almost forgot. Before you do that, I need you to say the magic spell. It's very important."

"What magic spell?"

"Five words. Can you remember five words?"

"I think so."

"Okay, then. Here are the five words: Death will turn into life. Can you say that? Death will turn into life."

I looked at him and then the hat under which Whiskers, his crushed skull seeping blood and brains, lay. Slowly, I said, "Death will turn into life." Then I tapped the hat three times, just like he told me.

"Now then," he said, picking up a flashlight and waving it above the hat. "Lift up the hat."

With great trepidation, I placed my hand on the brim of the black bowler's hat and slowly lifted it upward. I peered beneath the hat and saw the rabbit, Whiskers, only now he wasn't bloody. Only now he wasn't dead. He looked at me with those big black eyes, nose twitching once again, and I could barely contain myself.

"Whiskers!" I said. "He's alive! I made him alive!"

The magician laughed. "Indeed you did!"

Now, when I looked around, I saw that there were dozens of people again, and they were all smiling and cheering and clapping. Had they been here the whole time?

"And my boy," he said. "If your parents give you permission, I would very much like it if you would take Whiskers home as a pet."

More cheers and applause. My mother and father and sisters were among those that were cheering. I turned toward them.

"Can I?" I said, wide-eyed. "Can I take Whiskers home as a pet?"

My father looked at my mother, and my mother looked at my father. Then my father nodded his head and said, "It's very kind of the magician. Yes, you may have a pet. We're happy to welcome Whiskers into our house."

I jumped up and down with joy. To this day, it is still one of the greatest moments of my life. The magician handed me the rabbit and smoothed my hair with his hand. "He'll make a great pet. I'm sure you'll love him."

And so I took the rabbit home and made him my pet. He

sure was a sweet little fellow. But Whiskers didn't live very long. Maybe three weeks and then his body stiffened and he stopped moving. I cried and cried. My father buried him in the garden, and I wondered for a long time if he would come to life again, but he never did.

CHAPTER 24

It was Chief Mickel who finally pushed for my release. He said that certain mistakes had been made by the department. Certain possibilities overlooked. And the judge, a hefty fellow with a God-like beard, agreed with him. He scolded the attorneys on both sides. Scolded the investigators. Said that it was an embarrassment that an innocent man had spent even a single day in prison. Then he looked me in the eyes and, with a voice both grave and paternal, said, "A simple apology will never be enough for the pain and suffering you endured, Mr. Greiner. It will not make up for the days of your life stolen. But, unfortunately, it's all I can offer. That, and your release from prison."

And just like that I was a free man, having served eleven months in prison. I walked out of the courtroom, and I didn't know what to feel. You'd think I would have been happy, but I wasn't. I'd become psychologically prepared to spend the next twenty years behind those bars. Maybe I was just shell-shocked.

My mother was outside the courthouse waiting for me in her truck. The same truck, I thought with grim irony, that she'd used to move Chloe's body. When she saw me, she didn't honk the horn. She didn't smile and wave. She didn't get out of the truck and embrace me. She just rolled down the window and said, "Lizzy's dead. Set herself on fire."

I said, "I know." Then I kept walking. Mom shoved the truck in gear and drove alongside me for a while, but I didn't look up.

"Let me give you a ride," she said. "I'll take you home. I'll make you a home-cooked meal."

I just shook my head. I said, "I don't want a ride. I'll find my own way. And your house isn't my home. Not anymore."

"Maybe not," she said. "In any case, I'm glad you're free."

"Nobody's free," I mumbled.

And that was that. I kept walking and Mom stopped following. I took a bus into town. There I went to the bowling alley and bowled a couple of games, concerned not with how many pins I hit, but with how hard they went down. Then I went to the Manhattan Bar and had a couple of drinks alongside an old woman and her father. The drinks only made me feel worse. As I slugged down a final bourbon, I decided what I was going to do.

The sun was setting as I made the long walk through town and toward Nicole's house. I stood in front of the house with my hands buried in my pockets. After a year, nothing had really changed. The same blue welcome mat was on the porch. The same wind chimes clanging menacingly. I took a deep breath and rang the doorbell. Nicole was the one who answered. Her face was scrubbed clean of makeup and her hair was a mess. I thought she looked beautiful. Before she could even say a word, I dropped to my knee. I said, "I'd like you to marry me. That's what I'd like." I didn't have a diamond ring. It was poorly conceived. Still, she covered her mouth with her hands and nodded yes. I rose to my feet and we hugged and kissed. Soon her parents were there, and her brother, and they pretended like they were happy, but I knew they weren't.

Two months later we went to the courthouse and things were settled.

Years go by, some of them quickly, some of them not. There were many times where Nicole and I thought about leaving Leadville, but we never got around to doing it. After all, where would we have gone? Eventually, I got a job at the Climax Mine, shoveling and digging all day, just like my father did and his father and grandfather before him. I always figured there must have been some sort of metaphorical significance, but I could never figure out what the hell it was. Nicole, meanwhile, got a job at the school, teaching preschool. She was always real nurturing and liked kids, so the job suited her well. Three years after we got married, she was pregnant. That's the way these things go. She gave birth to a boy, and we named him Tanner. He has brown hair and blue eyes. I pray he doesn't take after me. I pray that he leaves the mountain.

From the time he was old enough to listen, I've been telling Tanner the story of the Lantern Man. About how his ghost wanders through the forest each and every night. How he whistles a single note, unchanging. How he searches for children who have strayed too far from the path to keep him eternal company in his cold, abandoned tunnel. I've also told him how the Lantern Man killed both of my sisters. One by water. One by fire. The stories scare him. He has a lot of nightmares.

Nicole, for her part, has never liked the stories. She says that children have enough to be scared of without their parents adding to their internal terror. She says that I need to move on from the past. That instead of always swimming in the darkness of yesterday, I should focus on the life I'm living now. A life with her. A life with Tanner. I wish I could, but it's not realistic. The traumas I experienced, that my whole family experienced, will always define who I am. And so, I share those traumas with my son. Because he needs to know who I am, what I've been through.

Of course, there are times when I wonder if it was really me who lived through those dark days or if it was only a stranger who shared my name and skin and blood. Some of those days and moments I remember clearly, but others remain indistinct, like mountain peaks through the encroaching fog. For example, I have almost no recollection of that awful day when Shannon was pulled beneath the surface of the water, never to gasp again. Or that night when Chloe was murdered, shards of skull buried in the snow. I know those horrific occurrences happened, and I know I played some part in both of them, but when I try remembering, the images are too blurry. It's strange. Why can I remember, with astounding vividness, days from my childhood with no apparent significance, while those defining moments seem to vanish into the dark and mist, never to be touched or tasted again?

CHAPTER 25

One evening, late summer, I was in the house by myself (Nicole and Tanner, perhaps looking to relieve themselves of my gloomy and drunk company, had gone to a friend's house for the evening). I sat in the kitchen and drank beer and listened to the rain pattering against the asphalt. It was shortly after nine o'clock and I had just dozed off, my hand still gripping my Budweiser, when I heard a soft knocking on the front door. At first, I thought it was just a part of my dream, and I remained where I was. But then the knocking became louder and more persistent. Somebody was at the door, and I couldn't imagine who.

I managed to get to my feet, my head spinning from beer and exhaustion. Through the kitchen I staggered and toward the front door. More knocking. I peeked through the peephole. A man stood there, getting soaked in the rain. He wore a pea coat and a newsboy's hat. His head was angled down so I couldn't see his face. "Who is it?" I shouted through the door, but the answer was muffled. I didn't have a gun, didn't have a blade, but I wasn't scared. I opened the door. The man looked up. His face was creased and weathered. His lower lip was quivering. His eyes were bloodshot. It took me a moment to recognize him.

It was my father.

He nodded his head, said, "It's been an awful long time, son."

No anger, not yet. "Yes," I said. "It has."

He wiped the rain from the brim of his cap. "Can I come

inside? Just for a while. I have some things to tell you. Some things you ought to know."

Some things to tell me? For some reason, I laughed. The world was sick and there was no cure. I shrugged my shoulders and moved aside. My father entered the house.

I had a sudden urge to spit on him. After all, he'd abandoned me, abandoned all of us. But, no, I couldn't spare the spit. Instead, I just stood there, staring at him, and eventually, he moved to the couch and slumped down in the corner. I remained standing, my arms folded. In the flickering light of my broken floor lamp, he looked extraordinarily old and frail, even though, if my math was correct, he wasn't yet fifty. It didn't seem real, him sitting on my couch, staring at his own calloused hands. Instead, it seemed like a blurry dream from which I would soon be shaken awake. More than a decade had passed since I had last seen him, since I had last spoken to him. And still, I had no desire to hear what he had to say. No desire to tell him what I thought. He wasn't worth the effort. But then, he'd never been worth the effort.

"It's been a long time, Brandon," he said, which was also strange. He never called me Brandon. "I can only begin to imagine what you're feeling right now. I can only begin to imagine the resentment you must harbor."

Resentment? That was all he thought it was? I didn't respond; instead, I remained in the center of the room, my foot tapping on the floor. Whatever he imagined I was feeling, he was wrong. Because I wasn't feeling a thing. Only numbness.

He cleared his throat. "I understand that you got married to Nicole. Your high school sweetheart. That's good. She's a lovely girl. I also understand that you have a child. I'll bet you're a wonderful father. Better than I was. I'd like to meet him one day. Although I appreciate if you'd rather he not get to know his grandfather. I've got some work to do in that regard."

I was in no mood for his small talk. "What do you want, Dad?" I said. "I don't have all night. I'd like you out of here before my family returns."

Now he leaned back on the couch and nodded his head slowly. His mouth opened and then closed and then opened again. "Yes. That's fair. I'll get to the point. I want to tell you the truth. About your sister, Lizzy. About what happened to her."

And now, I could feel the rage beginning to rise. But, no. I wouldn't allow that to happen. He wouldn't cause those emotions inside of me.

"You want to tell me what happened to her?" I asked. "There's no need. It's already public record. She burned in a fire."

He blinked a few times, as if trying to get a better look at his son or, perhaps, his son's soul.

"Yes, the fire. I'll get to that. But first, I would very much like a drink. Can you get me a drink?"

My jaw tightened. "A drink? You want a drink? Sure. Why the hell not? What do you want? A sipper of gin? Tequila? How about some Windex?"

He chuckled and shook his head. "No. I don't do that anymore. I'm a changed man, see. No more booze for me. How about a glass of milk? With an ice cube. Is that something you could do?"

And now I smiled. It *was* a dream. My old man. In my living room. Asking for milk. With an ice cube.

"Sure. Anything for you, Dad."

I went to the kitchen and poured his glass of milk. Then I pushed an ice cube out of the plastic mold and dropped it in the glass. I grabbed myself another Budweiser. I didn't like drinking, never had. But outside the rain fell, and my mourning would never cease.

I returned to the living room and handed him the milk. He thanked me and then placed the glass to his trembling lips. He drank quickly, the milk streaming down his chin. I watched him with measured contempt. He finished in just a few seconds and then wiped his mouth with his sleeve. I twisted open my beer and took a single chug. Then I stared at him and nodded my head deliberately. "Okay," I said. "Speak."

"Yes," he said. "I will. But first, I want to tell you something else. I want to tell you that you should know that I never stopped loving you. And that I'm sorry for leaving. I shouldn't have. I was wrong."

"Speak," I said again.

He nodded his head wearily and gazed at his damaged hands. "Right. Then, where should we start? How about with Shannon's death? The day she was sucked beneath the water. What you need to understand, son, is that after she was taken, my brain collapsed upon itself. Losing her was like losing the sky. I know you must have felt the same way. But here's the thing. Seeing Lizzy every day, the same face, the same DNA, only made things worse. It was too much for me. So I left."

"Yes," I said. "You left. Tell me something I don't fucking already know."

"Please. Give me a chance. I know it was wrong. I know I was being a coward. I got in my car and drove. Never said goodbye. I made it as far as Nevada. I ended up in a little shithole called Boulder City. It was just what I needed, though. A place where I was anonymous. A place that was far away from all the sadness and rage and confusion of Leadville. For several months, I lived in this cheap little motel. The kind of place where they didn't ask any questions about who you are or where you come from. I made money at the filling station and, later, at the landfill. I also got involved with this woman. Sheila was her name. She wasn't very pretty. Wasn't very smart. Wasn't very lucky. She'd been in and out of jail for the last couple of years for drugs and prostitution and check fraud. That kind of stuff. But she was a good woman. Showed me compassion. She asked me about my life. About all of you children. And she encouraged me to go back home. To make amends. For a long time, I refused. But she wore me down. So eventually, I did. Go back, I mean. But it was too late. By the time I made it to Colorado, the girl was already dead. And you'd been charged with killing her."

My father closed his eyes for a few moments and then opened them. Such sadness and resignation in those eyes. He rose from the couch and walked across the room. He pulled the curtain back from the window and stared at the rain falling on the darkened yard outside. When he spoke again, his voice was low and quiet. I had to strain to hear him.

"I would have gone and seen you in prison, but I was too ashamed. Not for the things that you'd been accused of, but for the fact that I'd left you and, perhaps, in some way, been the cause of it all. As for your mother, well, there were other reasons that I didn't go and see her. None of them justified. But Lizzy. I did see her."

This surprised me, but I remained cool. Indifferent. "Okay," I said, shrugging. "So you saw Lizzy. So what?"

"I'm getting to that. Just listen. I called her on the phone. She wasn't happy to hear my voice, as you can imagine. But she didn't hang up. I could tell that she was devastated. Could tell that she was lonely. Finally, after some prodding, she agreed to meet me. She wanted to meet at the cemetery. In front of the plot where Shannon was buried."

"Please," I said, my fist clenching. "Don't desecrate Shannon's memory. Not now."

"I'm not trying to desecrate anybody's memory. Let me speak. When I got to the cemetery, Lizzy was already sitting on that bench, as if she'd been waiting for me her whole life. I sat next to her. For a long time, neither of us spoke. In fact, she wouldn't even look me in the eyes. But then, as the snow fell softly, she started crying. I pulled her close and we huddled there together. She was filled with such pain. I guess all of us were. Soon, she started talking. She talked for a long time. And she told me everything."

She told me everything. I shivered. Then I took a long gulp of my beer. "Everything? What does that mean? What, exactly, did she tell you?"

My father sighed deeply, his eyes closing momentarily. "Well, she started by telling me about the letter she wrote. Why she'd done it. At the time, she was furious with you. That you'd go back to Nicole. She felt as if you'd abandoned her. She hadn't planned on mailing it, of course. But for some reason, she did. Motives aren't always easy to understand."

"I never abandoned her. Never."

"I know you didn't, Stormy."

"Nicole had nothing to do with the way I felt about Lizzy. I wish she could have understood that."

"I wish that, too. Anyway. What she told me next, shocked me. I wasn't prepared for it. You see, she told me you were innocent. Said that you had nothing to do with that girl's death. She was adamant."

"Yes. She was right. It wasn't me."

"I asked her how she knew that. How she could be so sure. And then she told me what happened. What really happened. She told me how she'd followed you that night. How she saw you making love to that girl—"

"That's wrong. I never—"

"How she waited until you left, all the while the rage building up inside of her. She hadn't planned on hurting her, son. She really hadn't. She grabbed a rock. And then..."

I could feel the tears welling in my eyes. "Lizzy. She was a good girl. She never—"

My father rubbed his eyes. Was he crying, too? "All of us are murderers, Stormy. I've always believed that. Under the right circumstances. When the moon shines just right."

"I loved Lizzy the most. I should have told her more often."

Another sigh from my father. "Something else you should know. It was always the letter that she felt most guilty about. More so than killing the girl. It was the letter. She'd betrayed you. It was more than she could live with. She knew she needed to make it right. And so, once she finished spilling her guts, she told me that she was ready to go to the police and confess. For everything. Not because she feared God's wrath. But because she wanted you to be free. She loved you, Stormy. She loved you so much."

I rubbed at my eyes before taking a final chug of my beer and placing the bottle on the floor. Then I started pacing across the living room, pulling my hair back with my hand. It was all wrong. A sudden burst of anger, and I slammed the wall with the palm of my hand. I wanted to hurt somebody. With all the violence in my soul. But, no. I took a deep breath. Then another.

"Okay," I said. "So she wanted to confess. Then why the fuck did she wait so long? And why didn't she just go to the cops? Why'd she fill up those goddamn journals instead?"

My father answered right away. "So they'd think she was crazy. That's why."

"Why'd she want that? I don't understand."

"I'm getting to it. I'll explain it all. But first I need another drink. And let's make it beer this time. No more goddamn milk."

CHAPTER 26

I went back to the kitchen and grabbed two beers. Then I grabbed two more. Just to be safe. I popped open the first two and handed one to my dad. He drank his beer quickly and so did I. I opened two more. And then we both sat down, this time next to each other, on the couch.

"Anyway," my father said. "That night at the cemetery. I did my best to talk her down. I told her that no matter how much we wanted to, we couldn't fix the past. And I told her that, no matter what, she couldn't confess. Not in the way she was planning to, anyway."

"Couldn't confess?" I said, my voice rising. "Why the hell not? You wanted me to rot in prison for her sins?"

"No, Stormy. That's not it at all. It's just that I couldn't bear to have one child released from prison and another placed inside. I'd already lost too much. Surely you can understand that. So...I came up with a plan. An outlandish one. A plan to get you released. And a plan to keep Lizzy free as well."

I clenched my jaw. Everything was jumbled. "A plan? You're talking about the journals?"

My father sucked down the rest of his beer and then reached into his shirt pocket and pulled out a can of Copenhagen. He snapped the can against his thigh a few times before opening it and taking a healthy pinch. He placed the tobacco between his lower lip and gum and then spit a brown stream of saliva into his empty bottle.

"That's right. The journals." And now he smiled. "I'm not good at much. You know that better than anybody. But I am good at telling stories. And so that's what Lizzy and I would do. We'd write a story. A story with twists and turns. A story with enough intrigue to keep the authorities engaged. But with enough truth to keep them believing."

I shook my head. "You've lost me, Dad."

He grabbed my thigh. "Just hold on a second. I'm getting to everything. Let's start with the Lantern Man. You remember him? Of course, you do. Remember how fascinated Lizzy always was with him? From the time she was a kid, she'd drawn pictures of him. Wrote stories about him. But that was all fiction. Creativity. For this narrative, we needed something different. Evidence of her deluded perception. Her hallucinations. Schizophrenia, maybe."

"Schizophrenia? But—"

"Of course, we never expected the real-life Lantern Man to make an appearance. This Horst Fischer. That was unexpected. Detective Buchanan stumbled onto evidence that we didn't plant. Stumbled onto corpses that we hadn't killed."

I could feel my skin pulsing, and my vision was becoming fragmented. "I'm still having trouble following. So in Lizzy's story...in your story—"

"We thought it would be obvious. Anybody with an inkling of psychological insight would be able to see right through the narrative. They'd see that Lizzy suffered from mental illness. That the Lantern Man wasn't real. That it was she who killed Chloe. Hell, she nearly admits as much near the end of her narrative. And I quote: *Rage filled my throat, causing me to choke. I grabbed a rock that was nearby. With the devil guiding my arm, I came down hard, smattering her skull into eight identical pieces. Still she breathed and still she crawled.*"

My father was speaking quickly now. I tried to slow him down. "So let me get this straight," I said. "Just to be clear. The two of you spent all this time—what, weeks, months?—working on this story. A story that would show Lizzy to be a fucking nut case. That would show her to be a murderer. You placed the journals in some sort of a fireproof box, ensuring that they would be recovered. And after the authorities read the journals and did their new investigation, you figured I'd be released."

"And you were."

I scratched at the skin on my cheek and clenched my jaw. "But it still doesn't make sense. Lizzy. You said that she would be free, too. But she fucking died. What kind of a plan is that? What kind of a story is that?"

My father spat another stream of tobacco juice into his bottle. Then he looked at me with a mischievous glint in his eye. "A beautiful story," he said.

A beautiful story? Was he also delusional? Just like Lizzy had been?

"Don't you see, son? The Lantern Man served another purpose. A far greater purpose."

"I'm not following."

My father's eyes narrowed to slits. "In the final scenes of Lizzy's narrative, beautifully written, we find her searching desperately for this boogeyman, this figment of her deluded mind. During the closing pages, in fact, she believes him to be waiting outside the cabin, ready to destroy her soul. But we, the readers, are clever. We've been given enough clues to know that this is all in Lizzy's mind. And we also know that she believes that fire is the only way to kill the Lantern Man. And so—"

"And so she lights the torch," I said. "And so she tries killing the Lantern Man by fire. But since he's not real...the fire spreads. Eventually, it consumes her."

My father smiled and nodded his head. "A tragic ending for our poor delusional girl. And a glorious work of fiction. You see, we needed them to believe that she had burned. It was the only way."

"Needed them to believe? So what you're saying is that she

didn't...I mean in real life—"

"No."

It felt as if my skin were strangling my soul. "You're not making any sense. Her body. They found it. They..." An image came into my head. Of the magician. Turning the dead into the living.

"They found a body, that is true. And she had Lizzy's DNA, that is also true. But every good story needs a twist, don't you think?"

And that's when I understood. I slumped down in my seat and closed my eyes. "No. I don't believe it. I—"

"Son, I'm a miner. I've spent my whole life digging. It was easy, then, going just six feet under."

"Then what you're saying is...is—"

"What I'm saying is that it wasn't Lizzy who burned in that cabin."

For the next twenty or thirty minutes, my father explained how they'd done it. How he'd paid the cemetery groundskeeper five hundred dollars for access and silence. How he and Lizzy had arrived at two in the morning and had spent several hours digging in the moonlight, while the snow fell and the wind blew. How they opened the casket and saw Shannon, face still lovely, arms folded over her chest as if she were just sleeping. And how they reburied the casket, now empty of a corpse.

The two of them carried Shannon's remains through the cemetery grounds and to his truck. They placed her in the bed and covered her with a tarp. They drove in silence as they made their way through the mountains toward Douglass City, the ghost town where Lizzy was supposed to be spending her final days waiting in delusional terror for the Lantern Man.

A person can only die once. That's how they reassured each other. They placed the corpse—my sister—inside the abandoned cabin. They left the journals, Lizzy's narrative, inside the fireproof box. They dressed her in Lizzy's clothes, Lizzy's shoes. They spread the floor with kerosene. And then...fire.

When the authorities found the body, there was never any doubt that it was Lizzy Greiner. After all, she had been reported missing. She'd been spotted by more than one eyewitness in the mountains, near Douglass City. The next day, my mother identified the body as Lizzy. And within several weeks, the DNA confirmed it.

Can you remember five words? Death will turn into life.

By the time he finished speaking, I was sobbing and yanking at my hair. "Where is she?" I begged. "Where's my sister?"

My father removed the wad of tobacco from behind his lower lip and shoved it into the Budweiser bottle. Then he rose to his feet. Outside, the rain had slowed, but the sky was lighted by distant lightning. He faced me and shook his head. "I don't know."

"What do you mean you don't know?"

"I gave her my car. Told her to drive far away. Told her not to tell anybody where she was going. Not even me. She said, 'What about Stormy? When will I see him again?' I told her that she had to wait. Five years at least."

"Five years? It's been a fucking decade."

"Yes. It has."

"Should I go looking for her? I bet I could figure out where—"

"It's a big old world, son. Better to wait, I think. Better to hope."

My father grabbed his jacket and his hat from the back of the couch. He put them on in silence. Suddenly, I felt panicked. I didn't want him to leave. I wanted to hear more stories. To comfort me. To scare me.

"Dad. When will I see you again?"

He looked at me, unblinking. "I'll be around."

"Maybe we can grab a beer sometime. Or even dinner."

"Sure, son. I'd like that."

But as he walked toward the front door, I knew it would never happen. I knew I would never see him again. Everything has to end. That's the shame about this world.

I opened the front door. Outside, the night was quiet and still. "Goodbye, Dad," I said.

He touched the brim of his cap. "Goodbye, Stormy. It was good seeing you. Even if it was only for a night."

And just like that, he was gone. And then I was crying again, and this time I couldn't stop.

CHAPTER 27

A month or two or three later. It was one in the morning, and outside the wind was moaning in anguish. I'd been awake all night, thinking, planning. Quietly, I got out of bed, leaving Nicole a million miles away. I got dressed in the darkness: jeans, flannel shirt, Carhartt jacket, stocking cap. Once outside, I loaded my trunk with a shovel and a pick axe and a crow bar. The moon was grinning in a blackened sky. I hit the engine and drove.

The radio was playing 1950s' do-wop, drenched with static. I gripped the wheel tightly. I reached into the glove compartment for my package of cigarettes, but it was empty. I crumpled it and tossed it on the ground. And now The Platters: *Yes, I'm the great pretender/ Adrift in a world of my own/ I've played the game but to my real shame/ You've left me to grieve all alone.*

Five minutes later, I parked a few blocks from Evergreen Cemetery. I didn't want my car to be spotted. I grabbed the tools and started walking down McWethy Drive toward the cemetery. Using a flashlight to guide my way, I pushed open the metal gate and walked along the path, listening to the soft mournful hum of souls forgotten.

I walked for some time until I came to the graves. Breathing heavily, I placed my flashlight on the ground. I moved until I was standing above Shannon's gravestone. Then I started digging.

The ground was hard, and even after an hour, I'd barely made a dent. Despite the cool temperatures, I was drenched with sweat, so I tossed my flannel and stocking hat aside. I thought about my father and sister digging through this dirt in the winter and had a hard time conceiving that it ever could have happened.

After conquering the first foot or so of dirt, the work seemed to become easier. My arms were aching, but the adrenalin allowed me to keep working. Three o'clock, and then four. Nobody else had entered the grounds, and all was quiet but the sound of my shovel slicing through the dirt.

The sky had begun to lighten, the stars fading into obscurity, when the blade of the shovel finally made contact with the casket. Dread, always dread, and I shoved aside the rest of the dirt. And now I stared at the casket, the wooden box where Shannon had been confined to an eternity and then some. All I needed to do was pry open the lid, and then I would see. If the casket was empty, then Lizzy was alive...

I stood there in that hole for a long time. I couldn't will my hands to open the lid. I sat down on the casket, my chin dropping to my chest. The world was a strange and terrifying place, I decided. I squeezed my eyes shut, and within a few minutes I was asleep.

I was awoken by the sound of somebody's voice. I opened my eyes, blinked a few times, and then looked upward where I saw an old man peering over the edge of the hole. "You okay?" he said.

I nodded my head. "Yes. I'm okay."

"What are you doing down there?"

It took me a moment to answer. "I needed to make sure that my sister is still dead," I said.

"And is she?"

"Yes. I think so."

"Need some help getting the dirt back on?"

"That would be much appreciated."

"All right, then. Come on out. Let's get busy."

I climbed out of the hole, my shovel dragging behind me. Once I reached solid ground, the old man didn't ask any more questions. He worked at the cemetery. He must have seen this type of thing from time to time. The two of us spent the next hour or so shoveling the dirt back on the casket. Once we were done, he told me that he'd take care of getting the gravestone properly planted.

I thanked him and went home.

CHAPTER 28

The other night, Nicole and I were sitting on the couch. Tanner was asleep. She was reading a magazine. I was staring at the ceiling. There was a crack, right near the light fixture. Every day it grew a micrometer or less. Nicole never seemed to notice. There was no need to tell her.

At some point, she stopped reading and placed her magazine on her lap. "I was thinking," she said.

"Yeah? About what?"

"About when we were kids. When we first started dating."

"That was a long time ago."

"I was thinking about when your sister, Lizzy, slept in my bed."

"Those were dark days," I said.

"Poor Lizzy was really struggling. I should have been more understanding. I'm sorry I wasn't understanding."

"It's okay. You've long since been forgiven."

A slight smile appeared on her face. She was still pretty, just as pretty as the day I first talked to her in the school hallway. "You know what the thing is?" she said. "Even after I broke up with you, you never let me get away. You kept after me. Trying to win me back."

"Yeah. I guess I did."

She was quiet for a few minutes, but I could tell that her thoughts were still back in that time. A decade ago.

"A few times you left flowers on my doorstep."

"Yes."

"You called every night."

"I did."

"I'm glad. I knew then that we'd be together. Eventually. Even if it took some time."

"Yes," I said. "I knew it, too."

Another pause. Then, "Something else I remember."

I turned my head toward hers. For some reason that I couldn't name, I felt a sense of dread rise in my chest. Her face was relaxed, though, her lips twitching into a Mona Lisa smile.

"It was just a few days after the incident with your sister. After I'd told you we couldn't be together. You came to my house. I was so conflicted then. I loved you, I really loved you, but my parents, they had convinced me that it couldn't work. That you were too damaged. That your sister was too crazy. But on this night, they were gone. So, it was just you and me."

"I remember," I said. "I think I remember."

"I told you that you shouldn't be here. But I didn't make you leave. I liked you too much. We went up to my room. My whole body was trembling. I didn't know what to do. I remember we just stood there in awkward silence for some time. Then you told me that you loved me. I started crying. We were just kids. The next thing I knew, you pulled out a ring. And you asked me to wear that ring. Asked me to promise to be your girl. If not today than down the line. When things weren't so crazy. When our hearts could be free. And it was the most beautiful ring I'd ever seen. You told me it had been your mother's..."

I turned away from her. I had to. I stared at my hands. They were trembling.

"On that day, I told you no. I told you that we couldn't be together. Not today. Not ever. But in my heart, I knew. Of course, I knew. And then a couple of years later, you asked me again. This time to marry you. But this time without a ring. I've always wondered. Whatever happened to that ring, Stormy? It was so beautiful."

It was hard for me to speak, and when I did, the voice wasn't my own. "I stole it from my mother. When she was drunk. But it's gone now. Somewhere beneath the dirt. I don't know…"

CHAPTER 29

Last night I returned to Hagerman Tunnel. I don't know why. I don't know why.

It had been a decade since I'd taken that same walk: down Harrison Avenue, past the run-down brick buildings of downtown, past the mining ruins from the century before last, and toward the darkened crags of Mount Massive. Back then still a kid. Now I couldn't help thinking how each moment had been a new opportunity to turn around and go home; each moment a new opportunity for salvation. A billion individual moments. Each one wasted. Each one ignored.

This night, the stars and moon were out, the darkened clouds thin and transient, so I didn't have any problem seeing. I followed along the flat rail bed of an old narrow-gauge railroad and then came to a trail of long eroded train trestle. And then another trail, far rockier than the smooth rail bed, ascended steadily. I walked quickly, my breath heavy and my heartbeat quick. Another ten minutes and I saw the ruins of Douglass City, where once upon a time the Italian construction workers and jaded prostitutes were housed, now all granite rock and rotted wood and twisted metal. Then Opal Lake, the bone-white moon shimmering off its surface. I shivered, but not from the cold.

Even though the wind was blowing and even though the temperature was falling, I was now covered in a lather of perspiration. I kept walking. It seemed as if I'd been out here, in the darkness, forever. Twenty minutes passed. Thirty minutes.

Soon I spotted the sign for Hagerman Tunnel. *DANGER!*
DON'T ENTER! I thought of my sister. I thought of the Lantern
Man.

Then I thought of Chloe.

Naked. Staring right at me.

I stepped into the tunnel. The beam from my flashlight was
bouncing against the walls. I moved forward slowly, my body
dragged along by some unknown force.

Just another few steps and I fell to my knees. With my bare
hands, I quickly wiped away the snow and frozen dirt. *What are*
you looking for? Certainly not the truth. In my mind, an image,
twisted and blurry, of that girl, Chloe, her mouth frozen in an
eternal scream, her skull crushed to pieces. But not by the Lantern
Man. Not by Lizzy.

More snow wiped away. And then I spotted it, gleaming in
the light.

My mother's ring.

And on my hands, just a spot of blood, but it was spreading.

This morning, Nicole handed me an envelope. My name and
address were written on the front, but there was no return
address, no post office stamp. "I wonder who it's from," she said.
Without responding, I walked into our bedroom and closed the
door. I sat on the floor, beneath the window, and carefully
opened the envelope. I removed the piece of stationary paper
that was inside and flattened it out on the floor in front of me. I
took a deep breath and then read the letter, my mouth whispering the words.

My dearest Stormy,

And so the years fade away like forgotten souvenirs. But
please believe me when I say that not a minute passes without
me thinking about you. Not a minute passes where I don't

picture your smile, imagine your laughter. I miss you, Stormy. I miss you so much. I wonder if you miss me, too.

I recently learned that you got married. And that now you have a son. Does he look like you? Is he as caring and kind? I'll bet you're a great husband. I'll bet you're an even better father.

As for me, I guess I'm happy enough. I'm still drawing, still writing. I work in a little café, in a little town, far away from Leadville. I've made some new friends, and some of them make me laugh. They don't know me as Lizzy Greiner, though. You can understand. I've long since left behind my name, left behind my past. That was the choice I made, to save you, and I've never, not for a single moment, regretted that choice.

I still have hope in my heart that maybe one day we'll be able to see each other. That one day we'll be able to hold each other and talk and laugh and cry. But until then we can take comfort in our stories. We have so many of them.

And maybe those stories are all we ever really needed.

My heart with yours,
Lizzy

I refolded the letter and placed it back in the envelope. I sat there for a long time, staring at my trembling hands, thinking about all those souvenirs, lost. And even though, in my heart, I knew that my sister wasn't living a secret life in a faraway place, and even though the handwriting in the letter looked an awful lot like mine, I chose to cling to the illusion, as people are bound to do.

JON BASSOFF was born in 1974 in New York City and currently lives with his family in a ghost town somewhere in Colorado. His mountain gothic novel, *Corrosion*, has been translated in French and German and was nominated for the Grand Prix de Litterature Policiere, France's biggest crime fiction award. For his day job, Bassoff teaches high school English where he is known by students and faculty alike as the deranged writer guy. He is a connoisseur of tequila, hot sauces, psychobilly music, and flea-bag motels. *The Lantern Man* is his seventh novel.

jonbassoff.com

BOOKS

On the following pages are a few
more great titles from the
Down & Out Books publishing family.

For a complete list of books and to
sign up for our newsletter,
go to DownAndOutBooks.com.

Forgiveness Dies
A Trevor Galloway Thriller
J.J. Hensley

Down & Out Books
October 2019
978-1-64396-038-8

Upon being released after being incarcerated in a psychiatric facility, former narcotics detective and unlicensed PI Trevor Galloway has no idea how to begin picking up the pieces of his shattered life.

When he's hired to investigate threats against a controversial presidential candidate and handed a stack of photos that may hold all the clues, he finds himself racing against time, running from mercenaries, and holding on to his last shred of sanity.

Let It Snow
Nigel Bird

Down & Out Books
November 2019
978-1-64396-047-0

A police officer is murdered while talking down a suicidal teenager. A rhino is killed at the zoo and has its horn removed. The biggest store in the city is robbed by a mannequin and record snowfall has created chaos within the police department.

As detectives seek the perpetrators of these crimes, they reflect upon their lives. Each of them needs to make changes. Not all of them know where to begin.

It's going to be one hell of a Christmas.

Pavement
Andrew Davie

All Due Respect, an imprint of
Down & Out Books
978-1-948235-99-0

McGill and Gropper are unlicensed private investigators who operate out of a diner and do whatever it takes to get a job done.

When a trucker attacks a prostitute, her pimp turns to McGill and Gropper for protection.

But taking the job means crossing dangerous and well-connected criminals who will stop at nothing to settle the score.

Load
Preston Lang

Shotgun Honey, an imprint of
Down & Out Books
978-1-948235-04-4

Ana Luz is a wily Iraq War vet, getting by working at a laundromat and doing the occasional favor for a neighborhood drug dealer called Espada. Her mysterious boyfriend Cyril convinces her to rip off Espada and sell the product to one of Cyril's old friends out in Iowa.

On a high-speed chase from Manhattan to the flat heart of America, Ana Luz and Cyril find themselves pursued by corn-fed hustlers, Dominican gangsters, and some suspicious small-town cops. The couple will need all their cunning and muscle just to make one simple drug deal and come out alive.

CPSIA information can be obtained
at www.ICGtesting.com
Printed in the USA
FSHW020912280220
67521FS